T0287659

The Heart is Improvisational

An Anthology in Poetic Form

ESSENTIAL ANTHOLOGIES SERIES 11

**Canada Council   Conseil des Arts
for the Arts   du Canada**

**ONTARIO ARTS COUNCIL
CONSEIL DES ARTS DE L'ONTARIO**

an Ontario government agency
un organisme du gouvernement de l'Ontario

Canadä

Guernica Editions Inc. acknowledges the support of the Canada Council
for the Arts and the Ontario Arts Council. The Ontario Arts Council
is an agency of the Government of Ontario.

We acknowledge the financial support of the Government of Canada.
Nous reconnaissons l'appui financier du gouvernement du Canada.

The Heart is Improvisational

AN ANTHOLOGY IN POETIC FORM

COMPILED AND EDITED BY

CAROL LIPSZYC

GUERNICA
EDITIONS
TORONTO • BUFFALO • LANCASTER (U.K.)
2017

Copyright © 2017, the Editor, the Authors and Guernica Editions Inc.
All rights reserved. The use of any part of this publication,
reproduced, transmitted in any form or by any means, electronic,
mechanical, photocopying, recording or otherwise stored in a
retrieval system, without the prior consent of the publisher is an
infringement of the copyright law.

Carol Lipszyc, editor
Michael Mirolla, general editor
David Moratto, cover and interior design
Sue Lezon, cover art
Guernica Editions Inc.
1569 Heritage Way, Oakville, (ON), Canada L6M 2Z7
2250 Military Road, Tonawanda, N.Y. 14150-6000 U.S.A.
www.guernicaeditions.com

Distributors:
University of Toronto Press Distribution,
5201 Dufferin Street, Toronto (ON), Canada M3H 5T8
Gazelle Book Services, White Cross Mills
High Town, Lancaster LA1 4XS U.K.

First edition.
Printed in Canada.

Legal Deposit — Third Quarter
Library of Congress Catalog Card Number: 2017932205
Library and Archives Canada Cataloguing in Publication
The heart is improvisational : an anthology in poetic form / compiled
and edited by Carol Lipszyc.

(Essential anthologies ; 11)
Issued in print and electronic formats.
ISBN 978-1-77183-186-4 (softcover).--ISBN 978-1-77183-187-1 (EPUB).
--ISBN 978-1-77183-188-8 (Kindle)

1. Heart--Poetry. 2. Heart--Symbolic aspects--Poetry. 3. Canadian poetry
(English)--21st century. 4. Heart in literature. I. Lipszyc, Carol, editor
II. Series: Essential anthologies series (Toronto, Ont.) ; 11

PS8287.H43H43 2017   C811'.60803561   C2017-900587-1   C2017-900588-X

The Heart is Improvisational

AN ANTHOLOGY IN POETIC FORM

Contents

Introduction

IS IT ANY WONDER WE place on the heart, an organ so elemental and life-sustaining, the weight and accountability we do? Poets attribute an array of roles and capacities to the involuntary muscle in this anthology, as my introductory poem suggests. In the imagined and coveted heart, the weary and scorned heart, we store the grains of faith and the seeds of acrimony. The heart becomes a repository of erotic and familial love and a sanctuary for memory, which Kenneth Sherman reminds us the heart tenaciously fastens to. Painting in the flash and flare of red, the poets explore the flux of the heart's responses and instigations: the heart's tender overtures, its joyous pulse, its mating call for the other, its changeable temperament, its final tick in freeze-frame. And through the metaphors: clenches of the fist, blood river, tear of the scar, shovel that hits and buries the earth, species of birds, the poets evoke the charged catalyst of our storied lives.

My goal in sequencing the poems was to arrange a composition that modulates in tone and mood, its motifs running through the poems like musical riffs. I gathered poets who enjoy a wide readership with those who do not yet claim that visibility from both sides of the Canadian and American border. Europe is represented by one Portuguese poet, one Hungarian poet, and two poets from the United Kingdom.

I take the reader on a journey that branches out from the heart's historical and etymological roots in David Baker's and Susan Glickman's opening poems "Average Life" and "Cardiognosis" to Aimée Baker's visual projection of the heart in "Early Differentiation of the Body," which readies us for a more clinical perspective. Through that lens, in places medical practitioners and patients co-habit, Mindy Kronenberg, Kenneth Sherman, Kate Marshall Flaherty, Sue Rose, Elizabeth Arnold and Miriam N. Kotzin reveal how vulnerable and fragile we are, how dependent upon the muscular workings of the heart as it dispenses life in the poems: "Arrhythmia," "heart," "crimson," "L27011945," "Heart Valve," "Aviary," and "Flow Dynamics." In Tamar Yoseloff's "Donor," the ultimate sacrifice is made for the loved one; in meting out life, the giver is then drained of life. And although the miraculous heart that "[meets] the air" in Lorna Crozier's "Transplanted" has an appetite for living, it remembers all too well the trauma of its past.

The collection then portrays the bonds between parents and children at stages of the life cycle. We begin with Eva Tihanyi's two-line history of the heart that marks its beginning and end. Delving into the family domain, the unborn child's nascent love moves from the rhythm of the heart in Faith Shearin's "Love" to boundless parental love capsulated in Elizabeth Cohen's "Blue Bird," Susan Glickman's "When They Are Asleep In Their Nimbus Of Flame," Marilyn Bowering's "Love Poem for My Daughter," and Jerry Mirskin's "Love." Kate Flaherty weaves a portrait of an ever-nurturing mother in "Loop," while the adult regrets having worn a self-protective sheath against a widowed mother's need in the second of Sue Rose's poems "B02031929."

Poems that follow attend to the passing of loved ones in the family. Doug Rampseck invokes the heart-wrenching, fatal image of a father and the debris of earth in "Mud in Heaven," and Ellen Jaffe commemorates her cardiologist father as man of science, teacher, and magician of a kind. Ellen Jaffe then brings us to the final days of a beloved mother in "Flocking," softening her passing with the arrival and departure of birds who seemingly pay her homage.

Daniel Boland notes the celebratory yet fleeting nature of our lives in "A Birthday Poem." And the natural world, whether miniature or tree-tall, is omnipresent, guardian of its own spirit and heart in "Olympia Marblewing Butterfly," "Theoretical Chest," and Nirvana" by David Reibetanz, Doug Ramspeck, and John Barton. Drawing from Wordsworth's sonnet "The World Is Too Much with Us," M. Travis Lane asks in "Print" who "speaks for life" once illuminated through the owl's eyes. Elizabeth Cohen's "Lo, and Behold" answers back with a chorus of boisterous blue birds. These voices complement poems about the earth's capacity to restore our faith in "Poem on Good Friday," "L'avalasse," "Fisherman," and "Temple" by Daniel Boland, Jack Bedell, Sheryl St. Germain, and Kate Flaherty.

Place as reconfigured through the poet's eye pierces and probes the "swelling chest" "down past the bone" without a compass or marking on a map in Gillian Sze's and David Reibetanz's poems "Invitation" and "Open Night." Jerry Mirskin pays tribute to "Fiesole" and "Venice" when, at the epicentre of his partner poems, the duomo is "like a great tired heart" and Venice is "a valentine that says your heart is real / It seeks its other."

At the mid-point of the anthology, I have placed Campbell McGrath's "The Human Heart," testament to the organ in which we invest so much — the heart with which we hunger, the heart which we protect, build on, and imagine.

Erotic love and the memory of passion and romance in its prime occupy and complete the middle movement of the collection, At the head is "Inhabited Heart," Alexis Levitin's translation of the Portuguese poet, Eugénio de Andrade, followed in harmony with a sensitive and whimsical plucking of strings by Eva Tihanyi, John Barton, Michael Carrino, and Charles Fort. In her poem triggered from a magazine art cover, the late Malca Litovitz tells the graphic story of an archetypal bride and groom. The enchanted garden that Litovitz designs loses some of its floral charm when love waits in Michael Carrino's "In the Garden." The speaker in Robyn Sarah's "Scratch" waits too, still open for the "glow" and "tinder" that "jump start[s] the heart."

Alas, the past ushers in a place and time when love was unrealized in Faith Shearin's "Heart Island" and Carolyn Smart's "Crush." Remnants of love live somewhere between the living and the dead, among knowing ghosts and in the spirit of lovers who still seek closure in Ellen Jaffe's "Lost Heart Highway," Brynn Saito's "Match," Patrick Lane's "Assiniboine," Kim Maltman's "The Heart Falls Asleep," and Roo Borson's "Intermittent Rain." In Mary di Michele's "Possession is 9/10th of the Love," the widow dreams about her late husband in Technicolor, as the heart decrees, but the script is co-authored by the wizardly brain that transforms the golden hero into a stock, mustached figure of the silent screen. Oh, the heart recalls, Lorna Crozier chimes in, because the heart can't "sever its attachments" and so it dials up through the night as sender of love. If we answer, we land in the sensual, enveloping, unflinching heat of Jane Munro's "That empty house, your heart," or we are cast out to sea in the aftermath of lovemaking in Carol Lipszyc's "Buoy," before moving to a somewhat irreverent presentation of the heart.

We may aim to discipline the heart, but we will need to mediate and decipher the heart's conflicting demands, manage its incessant tapping, like that of an insubordinate, petulant child who opens and closes the front screen door on a humid summer night. In his sonnet "Heart," Donald Justice pleads with and chastises the "inseparable" organ, while Patricia Young questions why a heart can't summon up its youthful vigor in "Puzzle." Roger Greenwald's "Interlocutor" playfully discloses tension between the rambunctious, fearless right side of the heart and its self-satisfied counterpart. Trying to read the illegible text of the heart is fruitless, Rita Dove warns in "Heart to Heart," even as we offer ourselves to another. Giving completely of the heart can render us mute in Miriam N. Kotzin's "Turn." What has been inflicted and endured can close us off in Carol Lipszyc's "Slumbering

Woman," can embitter and deplete, burn to ashes in Beverly Ellenbogen's "Whittled Heart" and "Chamber." If that kind of loss isn't enough, we are prompted to acknowledge the heart's potential for violence, for its raw plunge into sexuality, for the fracture and the damage done in Eva Tihanyi's "The Heart As Lamb," Aimée Baker's "Night in the Arms of the Two-Hearted Lover," David Slavitt's "Raimon De Roussillion," Eva M. Thury's translation of the late Ernő Szép's poem "My Heart," John Barton's "The Tell-Tale Heart," and Michael Mirolla's "When We Lie."

The power of the heart continues to intrigue, confound and humble us. Matt Robinson mimics the Bard in his modern spin on the soliloquy. Should we split the heart's clattering in two? Steel ourselves against sharp-edged corners? Or ready ourselves for the possibility of ... and in mid-line, we turn the page and listen to the heart's irrepressible yearning. Hearts, animal or human, will not be contained in David Baker's "Mongrel Heart" and Charles Bukowski's "Bluebird." How can't we help but listen? Through the arc of a narrative poem and the journey of a life in Mark Brazaitis' "Two Countries," the young insatiable heart leaves room enough for the seasoned heart to comfort. And in the last sustaining musical passages, the coda, Eugénio de Andrade ascribes an enduring nobility and singularity to the heart that embraces life with passion, a life Lewis Turco reflects on in his poem "Body Parts," as he entrusts to his loved one an aged but eternally committed heart.

I wish to thank Michael Carrino for seconding and, at other times, clarifying my thoughts; my gratitude also goes out to Kenneth Sherman for first suggesting the heart as centerpiece for an anthology. Thank you, Michael Mirolla at Guernica, for believing in and contributing to the anthology and for being so prompt and helpful in answering my queries throughout the process. And now, I bring you what David Slavitt has called "my cardiac collection."

—Carol Lipszyc, Editor

The Heart is Improvisational

moth beating tan-scaled wings
on the porches of summer

chant of the whippoorwill
lit only by moonlight

soft vowel 'u' from the newborn's primer
'l', 'd' and 'b' in single syllable time

these are the sounds from the innermost chamber
these are the sounds that stem from within

river-barge heart
tows love's apprehension

four-valve diva bathed in red

sings to sing a circuit of desire

tender and insistent the pulse of its story
tender and insistent the story within

o heart of chambers and the span of wings
its elocution capricious

no cold metal ear can sufficiently hear

this poet in residence
tugging at the semblance of wondrous things

   Carol Lipszyc

Average Life

for Sheldon Zitner

In the OED
heart comes between hearse and hearth.
Cognates include heart-ache, heart-break, heart-burn,
heartless, heart's ease, heart-rending,
heart-whole and heart-wise.

In the embryo, it maps the species' evolution:
a tube at first, fit for a fish,
then two-chambered and frog-like,
then a turtle's unshelled three.

310 grams, no bigger than a fist,
it pumps 4,300 gallons a day,
beats 2 1/2 billion times
in an average life.

Eventually it may be replaced by a battery.
Barney Clark survived 112 days
on forced air and polyester; a baboon's heart
massaged Baby Fae
for three brief weeks.

Four red rooms
plush, and full of music
hiding in the chest's thicket.

Tap and listen:
is anyone home?

Susan Glickman

Cardiognosis

No less than Aristotle rendered first
the heart's interior as tri-chambered,
"the largest being on the right hand side,
the smallest on the left" (one thinks, whose left?),

"the medium-sized one in the middle,"
this from his *History of Animals*,
350 B. C. But Galen quarrels
strongly, with a gusto unusual

and blunt: "What wonder that Aristotle,
among his many anatomical
errors, thinks the heart in large animals
has three cavities!" This third ventricle,

he's sure, is just hollow space (*fovea*
in the Latin texts) in the right chamber.
Still, dispute over the interior
structures grows contentious. Avicenna

tries to resolve the conflict by putting
Aristotle's third chamber *into*
Galen's heart, "as it were, *between*" two
larger chambers, as by a graft, calling

this part the "non-ventricular meatus,"
which works as a storehouse for the pneuma
(*spiritus*) generated in it "from
the subtil blood." Thus, Mondeville's handy

diagram (1312), etched in his text,
places the third chamber at the heart's base.
Thereby Johannes Mesue displays his
heart-rooms not horizontally but stacked

vertically, then calls them "pouches as
some purses" have. Through the years, depictions
of the heart's outer shape evolve, fashion
by fashion, but always maintain these halves,

until every scheme leads to the deepened
cleft shape in the fourteenth century. It's
as if, as the heart's interior grows
fuller with possibilities, we find

its exterior grown pronounced by "dips,"
"dents," "angular indentations," until
the cloven heart becomes our given style:
three chambers inside a double heart-shape

within a single chest. It's irony
befitting a lover, beloved, and "that
which comes between them." The halved heart
wants a third. But here's the really funny

part. Vinken identifies an early
Coptic textile (c. 400) showing
a saint, "likely Ezekiel," looking
in the air — toward God, one assumes — and sees

floating there a small rust-colored shape, most
surely a heart, with a clear indentation
marking its top like the first valentine.
Yet close inspection shows it's not made that

way — not design, but long wear. It's a tear.

    David Baker

Early Differentiation of the Body

A Tyrolean farmer slaughters
a chicken only to find seven hearts
nestled deep beneath its fleshed
chest, but on the waxed grains
of the sonogram image
we learn that your single heart
originates under your chin.

Through the projection flicker,
landmarks begin to appear
with increasing clearness,
there your heart and the topography
of your head vaguely defined
and already a tendency
to become curled head to tail.

— *Aimée Baker*

Heart

So there you are at last,
on the diagnostician's screen,
fluctuating between clinical grey
and amber, chambers
opening and closing:
a mollusc
kneading its vital fluid.

You look so primitive.
Who would suspect you to inhabit
a human chest, to fasten
with such tenacity
onto memories, lyrics,
frames of an old black
and white film?

Hoarder, I lie awake at night
hearing you *thump thump*
as if you were banging on the door
of my life, pleading
for one more chance
to wipe the slate clean
and begin again.

— *Kenneth Sherman*

Arrhythmia

The needle on my doctor's chart
spins its erratic alphabet
across the fan-fold perforated paper.

My heart clenches a crooked bolt
like a mad conductor who grins, his rhythm
tipping over and around his podium.

All this time, a hidden tempest, the turmoil
and ecstasy dancing in my chest, sins
tripping virtue, the moon tugging and teasing

tides like lovers pulled from the waves
and tossed back. No wonder the breathless nights,
jewels of sweat draped on my back, the gasps for air,

and no one's there.

Mindy Kronenberg

crimson

red dust mountain
on planet mars —
ruffled collar of craters
crusted with dried magma
scabbing to points
like curled and rusted metal

i see this mount
Vesuvius
through a looking glass —

everything telescopes
at Emerge

into tiny tremblings
imperceptible as threads
in a Petri dish

chill air so stilling
a kaleidoscope
of metal gurneys
greens, sneakers and beeping
gadgets

everything microscoping
into this one gaping
puncture
angry blood congealing
into a rage of sore flesh

erect in shock

a hunch of open skin
screams for sutures

black stitch-thread
sterile
scissors lifeless on a tray

latex gloves snap
like some blue NASA frequency
on a distant monitor
black and white bug-static alien
in this vortex of volcanic
flesh erupting
sucking me into
its fiery core

⌒ *Kate Marshall Flaherty*

L27011945

Blood comes to the right atrium,
a survivor depleted, its hue cinereal,
needing the renewal of home.

Blood comes to the left atrium
freighted with life, a prodigal
returning, its pennant red as flame.

Blood comes to the right ventricle
stripped of properties, a livid stream
flowing to the lungs for revival.

Blood comes to the left ventricle,
bright with breath, its mission to redeem
with the aortic rank and file.

The healthy heart is impulsive,
an electric muscle the size of a fist.

⁓ **Sue Rose**

Heart Valve

They told me there'd be pain

so when I felt it,
sitting at my beat-up farm desk

that looks out glass doors

onto the browning garden — plain sparrows
bathing in the cube-shaped fountain

so violently they drain it,

the white-throats with their
wobbly two-note song

on the long way south still,

and our dogs
out like lights and almost

falling off their chairs

freed of the real-time for awhile
as time began for me

to swell, slow down, carry me out

of all this almost
to a where

about as strong a lure as love.

— *Elizabeth Arnold*

Aviary

My heart had become home
to Brooklyn's bright flocks of feral
parakeets flown from their perch
on freezing wires and winter-bare
branches. Left to themselves they
kept a noisy wordless communion.

Old women wrap themselves
in a rainbow of acrylic and fling open
their windows. They cover their sills
with crumbs and seeds, croon *budgie
budgie* to the empty air. Gone,

gone all the small sojourners, improbably
to roost awhile in the four dark
chambers of my heart. No heart can
hold a feathered riot long.

They flicked their tails and went, a merry
metastasis, a mess of molt and shit —
a grip of beak and claw.

I hold out my arm
and watch the clear cocktail in its slow
drip through the tube. We sit in a row,
each of us tethered breath by breath
keeping time.

⁓*Miriam N. Kotzin*

Flow Dynamics

So lightly and invisibly I hardly knew it,

river of blood descending without joy back to the heart
through the frail vein all that time

— the largest of the body! —

shredded then dissolved ("obliterated")
and there was a sudden seepage

into surrounding tissue

instead of the blood pouring out as you'd expect forever
and a new vein formed to bypass what was gone

like a wide meander

even the smallest flood ends, and the river
goes straight from that point.

But in my case the thin-walled base-ends held

forming an anabranch, a section of a river
that diverts from the main channel,

rejoins it downstream.

Local ones can be caused by or make
small islands in the watercourse

but sometimes they flow hundreds of miles

like the Bahr el Zeref in the south Sudan that splits from the
Bahr Al Jabal of the White Nile, doesn't return

until Malakal

instead of leaving behind,
as it could have with the blood being old,

a full-fledged oxbow lake

that before too long
will blister in the sun, become

a little blue scar beside the heart.

— *Elizabeth Arnold*

Donor

The prognosis is bad for you:
a heart clogged with the detritus
of living, grizzled and mottled,
purple and blue, so useless
it makes me love you more.

Have mine. I reach through
my sternum and into the cavity,
separate it from the aorta
and pulmonary artery. It is clean
ripe, ready to do your bidding.

It throbs in my outstretched hand,
a bird that has fallen from its nest.
Without hesitation, you accept.
It slips in neatly, warms to your body,
defibrillated by a single shock.

Easy. Your pulse quickens
with the thought of my sacrifice,
but my love for you has been drained
with my blood: I am
listless, cold to your touch.

Tamar Yoseloff

Transplanted

This heart met the air. Grew in the hours
between the first body and the next
a taste for things outside it: the heat
of high intensity, wind grieving
in the poplar leaves, the smell of steam
wafting through the open window
from the hot dog vendor's cart. Often it skips

a beat — a grouse explodes from brambles,
a man flies through the windshield,
a face the heart once knew
weeps in the corridor that gives nothing back
but unloveliness and glare.

Like a shovel that hits the earth, then rises,
and hits the earth again, it feels its own
dull blows. Some nights it is a sail billowing
with blood, a raw fist punching.
Some nights, beneath the weight of blankets,
flesh and bones, the heart remembers. Feels those
rubber gloves close around it, and goes cold.

Lorna Crozier

An Unabridged
History of the Heart

It beats.

It stops beating.

Eva Tihanyi

Love

You grew a heart right away
because you knew about chambers
and pumping and love. There
were months when the world saw
only me with a coat pulled close
to hide the beating of us. I couldn't
feel you moving though you moved
and you couldn't hear me speaking
though I spoke. We were blind to
each other: a potato and its earth.

Faith Shearin

Blue Bird

When I was twenty-two and heart-broken
I got the tattoo:

a blue bird over my right breast
I imagined was the place

that marked my pain.
Later I learned my bruised heart

was lower down
and on the other side.

But that bird didn't care, it has flown with me since,
over skin and blood, ribs and hips,

days of errands, dream-soaked nights.
It hovered over the death beds of each of my parents,

and for nine months it glided over the soft,
unconnected bones of my daughter's head,

it's left wing tilting from the top
of my nipple, up into the open air.

She often asks to see it now and when she does
I slip down my shirt, my bra, my mother pride.

I peel back my whole life so she can look
at mommy's bird, blurred and dipping now,

still flying across my body toward a place
where it will never arrive.

— *Elizabeth Cohen*

When They Are Asleep
In Their Nimbus Of Flame

the heart no longer asks for permission,
it loves what it loves. "Holy, holy!"
it exults over the chaste swell
of buttocks, the curve of shoulders
round in their sockets like eyeballs
scrolling the landscape of dreams;
like the pillowed heads, the knees flexed
against morning's exertions,
its staircases and adieux.

But when they are asleep they are wholly
here, cupped in my hands like sweet water.
My son, too old to bathe with his mother
whose limbs still remember that merriment, that
slippery grace. My daughter, who brushes away
her own tangles, and won't wear what I, longingly,
lay out. My husband, curled into himself —
boyish, startled, alone —
each one so alone in sleep.

The house groans and ticks through the lengthening night.
I drink tea, tidy things up, ask for permission
for a few hours more of this love.

   Susan Glickman

Love Poem for My Daughter

for Xan at fourteen

You are all the light in the world
gathered into a face,
your eyes deep space and stars —
who are you?
When you sleep, your breath stirs
the brooms of ages, dust shifts:
your skin is gold,
the past opens itself to your many dresses,
the night unravels its blue wool:
you stand on a far shore
about to set sail —
where are you going?
When you laugh,
the graves open, the dead put on makeup,
the souls of children wake up:
who will go in your company?
You are a stir of wind,
the scent of rare wood,
your mind mirrors the breath of sages,
your thoughts are new.
I called you and you came.
I loved you and you grew,
but who knew
this grace,
the wound flower in the heart's chain?

— Marilyn Bowering

Love

This one wants to climb the mountain
of snow in the parking lot, rather than *get in the car.*
I watch from behind the wheel.
His mountain is no Everest
no monument of grand sentience or avalanche
but one of those soiled mats, consumptive
with February rain. A declaration of nothing
in the sky-less terrarium of the mall.
Filthy, I think, bothered by his choice of mountains.
Though this isn't the first today.
There was the one downtown from which he rolled
like a tongue falling from an open mouth
while passersby looked at a boy on the sidewalk
lying fresh from the clouds.
And the one he polished off earlier this morning
which was better, as far as I could tell
as it rose naturally between our small house
and the dark pelt of pines in our backyard.
There I smiled to see him taking hold of his local kingdom.
This one is lesser.
Though he doesn't distinguish.
Ok, I say, after saying, *No, no.* Go ahead.
And when he gets to the top he turns
and waves to me, standing firm in his blue boots.
Calling and waving.
And I see, this is what he wanted.

And me?

My heart is in its cage. Pounding away.

⌣ *Jerry Mirskin*

Loop

my mother rocks by the fire   hooking a rose green rug   under kerosene glow

she holds her silver J   *poke and pull, repeat,*   the lamp's globe half full

knotted strips at her feet   coarse burlap on her lap   her glasses slip as

rock hook and hum   *rock hook and hum*   she retrieves lost strips

draws them to the light   little woolly heads   pop up in rows and whorls

she does this best   (not hooking but mending)   brings things to the up-side

whenever one of us kids   gets buried   she'll pull us through

mended   heartened   forgiven

⌒ **Kate Marshall Flaherty**

B02031929

It had been so long since she'd heard
the reassuring pace of another's heart
at her ear — she pressed her head
here, below my shoulder's hard
girdle and the soft upper of my breast,
and slipped into the worn rest
of the old, soothed by the serenade
of my heart, its secrets husbanded;

she'd slept alone in their double bed
for years, silence ballooning around her,
but I sat rigid, oppressed by her need,
when I should have hugged this woman
who once listened to my heart's patter
inside her, I should have stroked her head.

～ **Sue Rose**

Mud in Heaven

The mud in heaven must grow thick
with flies in summer. Celestial flies
that lift themselves above the tall
stink of grass. And what clings
to the bottoms of my father's boots
is holy as pig manure, damp and alluvial,
tracked into our mother's kitchen. And so
the smell of ammonia in the air, the sloshing
sounds from the bucket my brother carries
two-handed from the sink. Always the mud
and dirt that finds its way into the house —
field mud congealed with bits of stone
and hay and grass. Loose earth collecting
in windowsills and stairs, dust seeping
from bookshelves and overhead fans,
handprints smudging countertops and walls.
Everywhere grime gathering like the leaf
meal beneath our oak trees beside the barn,
the trees that empty themselves each fall
until they are bare skeletons, that make
of the earth their own dark decay.
And so our father's body, that fine salt of dirt,
unneeded now, loam that once was drawn
from the earth to make a man. It was in
our back field where we found him,
face down in the mud, a hand clutching
his chest. He must have climbed from
his tractor and made his way as far as the fence.
While our mother, not yet knowing, on
her knees in the kitchen, leaned her weight
into a blue sponge to make the floor shine.

⌐ **Doug Ramspeck**

If My Father Had Written Poems

He would have written about the heart,
describing the four chambers —
      right and left atrium
           left and right ventricle —
the vagus nerve, the valves —
pulmonary, aortic — and their tides of blood, systole
                            diastole
as he patiently measured high and low pressure,
EKG waves, reaction to stress.

He loved the names, loved teaching me
how they worked —
bringing home plaster models
      instead of valentines.

He put his passion into medical texts, not poems,
cut and pasted on the floor before computers.
I'd fall asleep to the click of my mother
      typing his papers.

Even off-duty, he listened for the syncopation
of irregular beats, slow murmurs —
      Benny Goodman, Duke Ellington,
Sarah Vaughan and Lena Horne —
their musical, emotional cardiology.

Unlike other kids' dads, mine knew magic —
he could massage dead hearts (like red-breasted birds),
coax them back to life.

I remember how he catalogued catastrophe:
      infarct
           thrombosis
                and cardiac arrest.

— *Ellen S. Jaffe*

Flocking

> *... A confession of birds*
> *flew overhead ...*
> — Ian Burgham, "A Confession of Birds," *The Grammar of Distance*

That Friday, four days before my mother died,
(cold and rainy for August)
birds flocked to the feeder outside her window
while she subsided deeper into her body,
not seeing
flickers, cardinals, blue jays,
mourning doves, goldfinches, nuthatches,
finally — just at dusk — an emerald humming-bird,
and then another.
Even the nurse's aide — pregnant,
wanting to get home to her toddler and pizza for dinner —
even she noticed: "Another hummer."

An instant, then gone, a green thought.

Were they there to see her off, messengers
from another world, fluttering
to take her ... ? "home" is the word that comes to
mind, though she didn't believe in an afterlife.

She would have welcomed these guests
shimmering beyond her reach,
the beating of hummingbirds' hearts
their insatiable hunger,
constant movement,
their capacity
for joy.

— *Ellen S. Jaffe*

A Birthday Poem

It is your own day again.

A happy, brief transit of the heart
that must, inevitably, slip through your fingers
like sand
and vanish at dusk
like the neighbor's cat
into the garden.

Every year you must try again
to catch it, pin it down
like a dazzling butterfly
an oriental kite
or some elusive Proteus
that might finally yield

a solar vein of gold.

But once again
it has already passed you
mutely rendered its stoic, numerical declaration
and moved on.

— *Daniel Boland*

Olympia Marblewing Butterfly

streaks of honey
knot the redwood of your wings
rosy marble soft enough to break
under the hug of skin you never wanted

inside a heart so small
even if it were stone
it wouldn't weigh
but I want to tell you that

you are heart the knot
a leaf rim
is all it ever took
to feel your way
to this bloodshot beauty

and nothing of stone is in you
no atom of the powder that lifts
you wind on wind is hard

even the way you skim the ground
tells how you know
the world is wing
that calls itself marble

is just as lighthearted
as you but
does not know it

— **David Reibetanz**

Theoretical Chest

The many someones have gathered
in this bright garden. An entire decade
has come out of the enclosed houses to go
down on knees and prune tomato plants.
In Rousseau's philosophy *amour de soi*
is preferable to *amour-propre*,
though these tomatoes are dangling
like hearts in the theoretical chest.
You think you are dreaming,
but then the body undulates as though
the wind is bending you like grass.
You think you are vanishing,
that everything you ever imagined
is sweating on this glass of lemonade
in the day's heat. Each time I believe
I see clearly what is topsoil
and what is clay, someone rings
the doorbell and sits down on the couch
and speaks in a hushed voice
about something I have never understood.
All I want tonight are lanterns to float
like votive candles on the pond
while I am sleeping, for the red heart
to be plucked like a tomato and placed
on this windowsill to ripen.

___*Doug Ramspeck*

Nirvana

Emily Carr, 1929

Whatever is held
inside the forest's coal-
dark heart was barely

carved into the felled
trees they raised
before the wood began

swelling with rain,
the finely wrought
distinctions peeling away

like stars from the sky.
The thickening grain
pushes the heart farther in,

readies it for the perfect
blankness between
darkness and light.

How I wish time
would stop,
the forest fall back.

I would carve all hearts
free of their prisons of rot,
hold them high in the sun,

their winged shapes each
a calyx of diamond
unfolding petals of light.

— *John Barton*

Print

Why should the wing marks on the snow
speak more of life
            (they speak of death)
than the gray path trundled bank to bank?

Getting and spending,
the waste is ours.
The owl's beak of indifference
upgathers us.

Our earnest, burrowing hours will leave
a nest of nits and gnawings so petit
one thaw will close it like a pore.

The pierced heart in its first
and last expression dropped
one tiny ruby, as if breath
were jewel only when it dies.

Who speaks for life?
The owl's eyes, too,
were "bright with it."

— *M. Travis Lane*

Lo, and Behold

Look at this:
a red leafed Japanese maple
filled with small blue birds
of an unknown genus.
A whole society of indigo life.

Red tree. Blue birds.
The branches blossoming
with pratter and preen,
An office of similarly clad secretaries,
each set upon some miniscule
and certain task.

There is not enough bandwidth in the world
to record such busy loveliness.
At least a 7.5 on the Richter scale of beauty.
It hurts the heart, really,
this explosion of song,
this flip book of life.

⁓ *Elizabeth Cohen*

Poem on Good Friday

An awakening, groggy earth
nurses its ice-wine hangover.

Its heart begins to speak in rivers and streams.

Craters and potholes have widened;
bleached, resurrected scraps of paper
fly like liberated avatars in the wind.

It's no wonder the Celts fell in love
with the Christian story
with all its rocks and thorns.

In the tawny grass
a few impossibly yellow and lilac crocuses
are splashing like sacred animation.

Raking must be done.
Taxes must be paid.
The tomb must be found
empty
so the swollen rivers can flow
and the robin can nest in the eaves.

Daniel Boland

L'avalasse

The old women of our parish
say such rain, *l'avalasse*,
throws sheets of sleep across your house
to wash away whatever burden
the day has brought. They walk outside
in their nightgowns as soon as the bullfrogs
stiffen in the ditch and hunker down,
believing the water will cleanse them of aches
and lighten the weight their years have built.

It's enough for me to step to the porch
with the dog to watch the backyard fill.
Inside, my wife and boys draw close
and breathe with such peace the house almost glows.
Their sleep is thick and well-deserved.
There's nothing worth waking them for
as long as this storm holds us to its heart.
I know the dreams they share will be enough
to keep us afloat when morning comes.

Outside, a murder of crows has landed
pecking its way through the mess this rain
has washed off our house into the grass.
Somewhere, the old women are bathing,
their lesson in the water coming down —
no matter how it pounds, this rain
will not outlast Noah's. Our land
is thirstier than his, our sins
much easier to wash away.

— *Jack Bedell*

Fisherman

To listen with hands and eyes
For the deep, unseen mouthing —
if I could have the faith of the fisherman
I would rip out my heart muscle,
sink a hook into its joyous pulsing,
sing it out on a long line,
and wait for the great dark.

— *Sheryl St. Germain*

Temple

Bengali yogi tips hands to lips,
a house made of people?
He stands in the sun, sinewy,
his white wrap stark
against his *caffa* skin.

A body is a temple, yes —
the cage of ribs
to keep the *anahata** heart,
two portals of breath,
two windows of light
and a long red welcome mat
for nourishment —
the dome of the crown in the clouds,
the root of the soles in the earth.

Yes, the body a holy place, a home:
    I ruminate,
      "we borrow these clothes ...
      light looks different
      on the stoop or the shrine ...
      but it is the same light."

A house made of people?

So many bones —
so many broken windows
and shuttered eyes,
so many human stones on this earth —

a house of people — impossible —
without love as mortar

and a cage of flesh and bone
to house
four luminous chambers.

— **Kate Marshall Flaherty**

---

*Anahata is the Sanscrit word for "heart", literally translated as "unstruck".

Invitation

One early morning
when the curtains rippled blue,
I looked down a row of trees to spot
a girl wheeling into the haloed street

and remembered the summer I followed
a beautiful face around the corner,
its cheeks not yet dusky
but all periwinkle and pledges.

Who knew how we wrung out each minute:
July was a place we thought we could stay.
One afternoon, we drove to where ditches
met dirt, and under a hot sun and salty hairlines,

you, hewn out of sky, reached out,
and a handful of wheat pierced my swelling chest.

⸺ *Gillian Sze*

Open Night

Buildings usurp the sky,
and the city's blackness foregrounds
gentle incandescents as they tie
night tight. Sirens and motors sound
below our roof garden. An ambulance screams
into this flushed spring evening so near
to the summer we will fill like a box with half-dreams:
the sky is quiet, the world full of fear.

Happiness is a black mug drunk down low,
or a glimpse of a proud woman drawing red hair
back behind her ears with both hands, slow,
or one final intake of this pine air —
when open starless night sounds its tone,
and probes your chest down past the bone.

⁓ **David Reibetanz**

Fiesole

I like the way they live forever in Italy.
I like the way they take the time to do it.
How they put their whole lives into it.
The wine will tell you this.
The way it stands on the table.
So lonely, dark and lonely.
I like the way they live forever in Italy.
Like each day they put a penny in.
A penny for art. One for work.
They know it will take a whole life to pay off.
All this art. All this beauty.
In Fiesole, outside of Florence
I saw two men walking the hills.
When they passed a small faded shrine
their walk faded. They gave a few pennies.
A handful of lira.
They were on one side of a hill
walking a small path to their homes.
On the other side was the city, and the duomo.
You can see it ten miles away
like a great tired heart sleeping soundly
in the smoke of sunlight.
Asleep and snug in the valley by the Arno.
Which side would I prefer?
From here we could see that the sun
was going down on one knee.
The grooves of the city were growing taller
like a taller garden.
Shadows were growing clever in the alleys.
Still, the sun was working hard as always.
Conspiring with the church and the city on one side
and the vine on the other.
I like the way they live forever in Italy.

⁓ *Jerry Mirskin*

Venice

The essence of which is a delta
of lovers unfolding their fans in the great square.
Or the painted gondoliers, standing unmoving
as the narrow streets and canals curl
in perpetual rendezvous. I waved at them
as they pimped their boats on evening's narrow skids.
The local angels, poised above it all,
stepping with hard shoes across dark water.
On foot we coursed from one smooth stone
to another, from doorway to square and piazza
and with each step seemed to go further within
as if toward an inner channel, a smoother stone.
Venice is a middle earth for honeymooners.
The light at night, luminous in its small golden cups,
a valentine that says your heart is real.
It seeks its other.
I walk behind you and take a picture
as you climb a small bridge to our true life together.
Do you remember the gondolier who let me sing my song?
The shutters that closed as I climbed into my better voice?
As we slid evenly on the narrow skids.
Day was entirely different.
I remember the Jewish ghetto on the northwest side.
The emptiness of the square, and the light
that illumined a tableau of men and cattlecars
suddenly soulless as dirt. And then inside
the museum, the remnants. A few candelabras.
A scroll. A decorated marriage contract
beneath which an old couple from Philadelphia
took our picture, and then left us alone.
And how with their going I felt so many absent,
until in that museum of loss I began to cave.
Do you remember how I pried at your clothing?
The thin veil of your blouse? Tugging at your body,
grasping for crease, for sensual curve.
Intent as I sank in that ungodly history
on mauling you for all you or I were worth.
Where were the golden cups of light?

The standing gondolier? The river of love?
I remember Venice. The wonderful food and wine.
The canals and the cave-like light among
the buildings, which was perfect at night.
And how I felt as a newlywed that I was entering
another life as we stepped into the fan of human history.
But mostly how I came to my senses
when, away from everyone, alone on the second floor
of the museum, you gently pushed away from me.
Out of modesty. Out of respect.

— *Jerry Mirskin*

The Human Heart

We construct it from tin and ambergris and clay,
    ochre, graph paper, a funnel
    of ghosts, whirlpool
in a downspout full of midsummer rain.

It is, for all its freedom and obstinance,
    an artifact of human agency
    in its maverick intricacy
its chaos reflected in earthly circumstance,

its appetites mirrored by a hungry world
    like the lights of the casino
    in the coyote's eye. Old
as the odor of almonds in the hills around Solano,

filigreed and chancelled with the flavor of blood oranges,
    fashioned from moonlight,
    yarn, nacre, cordite,
shaped and assembled valve by valve, flange by flange,

and finished with the carnal fire of interstellar dust.
    We build the human heart
    and lock it in its chest
and hope that what we have made can save us.

— *Campbell McGrath*

Inhabited Heart

Here are the hands.
They are the most beautiful signs of earth.
Angels are born here:
fresh, of the dawn, almost of dew,
with joyful, peopled hearts.

I place my mouth on them,
breathe their blood, a white murmur,
warm them from within, surrendered
in mine, the little hands of the world.

Some think they are the hands of god
—I know they are the hands of a man,
tremulous hulks where water,
sadness and the four seasons,
indifferent, filter in.

Don't touch them: they are love and goodness.
Even more: they smell of honeysuckle.
They are the first man, the first woman.
And now the dawn.

⌐Eugénio de Andrade
Translated by Alexis Levitin

My Heart Hears You Dreaming

Years pass but I do find you;
your open self is still my fate,
such joy your mouth is speaking.

I sight-read each day as it comes,
listen carefully to learn by beat
the song of your softest breathing.

And within the silence that is love,
my heart hears you dreaming.

I am friend not foe, a soul
who treads gently through
the griefs you've been keeping.

A lover who loves your fluent hands,
evening sky in summer:
your blue eyes simply being.

And though I am not with you now,
my heart hears you weeping.

Through the landscape of my fear,
I braille my way toward trust,
weary but believing.

Yet despite the journey I have made,
the music weakens,
the distance is not receding.

And within the silence that is love,
my heart hears you leaving.

— *Eva Tihanyi*

Let Your Heart

Dearest, let your heart be
the truth of you.

Forget the world's conclusions,
forget fear.

Behind you now:
the long years of longing.

Forget them.

Let desire, which you speak
so fluently, with such unnerving eloquence,
be your first language.

If you trust your body to dance,
it will.

—*Eva Tihanyi*

Naked Hearts

Avec un coeur nu dans ton coeur rempli,
I will live,
the body's audacity to be learned,

meeting the first evening,
fingers linking somewhere along Saint-Denis.

Shall we stop at Café Nelligan
and drink in the warmth
of candles and mulled wine?

Or shall we walk on

until our eyes meet,
until each insinuation of the flesh

spins us closer,
our gradual skins flowering
with slow desire?

Cross this threshold with me,
discover how deeply the city sleeps.

No one hears us reduce
ourselves to bodies changing
shape in the vivid dark.

The grief of our bodies
retells the world's body of grief.

Draw me between your thighs,
into the search
of mouths, the orifices of love.
Listen to the soft cadences of my sighs.

I had forgotten how my grief
rises, how quickly it wells up
under the tongue's roughness.

Release it, nest in my arms.
Lying here,
the earth is caught in a split-second calm.

I no longer fear to be a man
and we are lovers whether our lovers
are women or men.

Avec un coeur rempli dans mon coeur nu,
lie beside me.

In this century those like us
refuse like us
to live as if we have never been.

⌐ *John Barton*

The Request

My bedroom is white with lilies and gladiolus,
yellow and red roses. Fire eaters and Flamenco dancers are everywhere
on Canal Street, haphazard and narrow, with old women hawking ice cream.

Sweet Darlene, please swing by and pirate my heart.
Forget your rosaries, your social ramble.
My bedroom is white with lilies and gladiolus,

yellow and red roses. We could doze and listen
to Mr. Gonzalez inflate crepe paper falcons.
On Canal Street, haphazard and narrow, with old women hawking ice cream

everyone is not as chic as the Arabs and Brazilians
riding the streetcars in high heels and perfect hairdos.
My bedroom is white with lilies and gladiolus,

yellow and red roses. We could gaze at the filigree
wall as the sunset distills fire eaters into bears eating berries
on Canal Street, haphazard and narrow, with old women hawking ice cream.

Sweet Darlene, visit me. Make this afternoon dangerous
as bears nearly dancing and spilling berries out of heaven.
My bedroom is white with lilies and gladiolus
on Canal Street, haphazard and narrow, with old women hawking ice cream.

⌒ *Michael Carrino*

Valentine

When was it that we last saw each other?

When we met I was half-in-love with you.
My heart-shaped scar was your Valentine,
a flask of moonshine, meth-mints, and corn raves.
You gave me your breath and I gave you my own.
We walked under the arc of human color
and you held my arms as if you never wanted
to let go of this needful widowed man.
When we met I was half-in-love with you.
You gave me your breath and I gave you my own.
Years writing from the light of my body
I finally sent you my last book of poems.
You danced without music or men
as train wheels made the buffalo stampede
and jump their bright hula-hoops of desire.
Was it love at first sight, your Irish eyes,
Eros and bottled fire, extinguished,
saved by Brown Zorro in a ragged cape?
You gave me your breath and I gave you my own.
When we met I was half-in-love with you.

— *Charles Fort*

We Kissed As Lovers
Under Widowed Light

We kissed as lovers under widowed light
and cradled the captain's last vow and wed.
The animals fled and the blowers bloomed.

We pulled ourselves from the wishing well
that had tied hell closer to the heavens.
We kissed as lovers under widowed light.

Had the brown stars shifted across the sky
into a kaleidoscope of the heart?
The animals fled and the flowers bloomed.

There was a pendulum and crescent moon
children walking on the breaking ice pond.
We kissed as lovers under widowed light.

They discovered signs of life this evening
found in the threadbare apparel of death.
The animals fled and the flowers bloomed.

They offered us the gift of first refusal:
land on our feet or float in mid-air.
We kissed as lovers under widowed light.
The animals fled and the flowers bloomed.

⌐ ***Charles Fort***

The Hearts

After a New York cover, February 12, 2001

Ace of Hearts,
you wake up alone:
hand on pelvis,
fist of the warrior,
waiting.

Two of Hearts,
you hold your heart
in your hand,
a bag of candy
offered to the first passerby.
The bride is nowhere to be seen;
then, she eats your kiss,
a jujube,
throws you away.

Three of Hearts
on bended knees.
Romeo woos
in the garden of love,
while the bride's heart stands
on the precarious ledge,
leaning.

Four of Hearts,
the groom comes out
on the balcony and growls
for you to leave,
take your floral heart
with you.
The bride cranes on her long legs,
bending her head to you,
but not moving.

Five of Hearts,
smiles
holding the secret heart of love,
while the groom
furrows his brow,
stands on the edge
of the balcony.

You are happy now
on both knees,
the heart of your love
flowing above your head.

Six of Hearts,
an odd assortment —
you pirouette in the foyer,
and the angry groom
leaps down to grab your neck.

The bride hovers above you,
frightened for you both,
but secretly relishing
her hidden power.

Other loves
stand point at your ardor —
you hold your heart, a mirror.

Seven of Hearts:
a duel,
Your face almost feminine
next to the glowering, swirling brow
of the groom.
Your pistols are purple,
the guns of Israel —
they shoot
into the ether.
Five of us stand to watch you,
but your beloved is home
safe in bed.

Eight of Hearts
an aria rises out of the heart of the groom you slew.
Despite your gentle demeanor,
you have knocked the man flat.
A gaggle of hearts surrounds you in your triumph.

Nine of Hearts,
the bride speaks:

At our wedding,
second husband of mine,
a chorus of red roses
stings in the upper pew
at Cambridge.
The priest wears his heart
on his head
and reads from Kahil Gibran.

Ten of Hearts —
an expanded circle.
The wife is pregnant with your eighth.
Your arms
do not reach around
her expanded waist.
They circle the globe,
various degrees of smiles
on the faces of your children.

The circular movements of heart:
the hips, the arms
in their natural rotation,
the way the seasons come and go
in the garden.

— *Malca Litovitz*

In the Garden

Tonight, prostrate on the couch
I'm waiting in the hanging gardens
for the Contessa. She is late and I pace,
stare past the anchored sailboats pulling
at the bottom of the bay. Where is she?

When it's deepest, love is forgetful. It dries
the mouth and wilts
the heart. I want her
to believe this when she arrives
and I methodically cover her
silk scarf with well-placed kisses, whispering:
you must keep track of time.

But this daydream has teeth. The Contessa
lives inland — teaches school,
her jasmine-scented fan locked inside the desk,
while I lie here; a winter wind
intrudes. Which way
does it blow today?

This life is a series of clues
without a mystery. My response,
an embarrassed shrug, a kiss
on her damp cheek, her eyes
composed under the cool white towel
I pat us dry with, after bathing
before strolling in the gardens, exploring.

⌒ *Michael Carrino*

Scratch

The tinder words, where are they,
the ones that
jump-start the heart —

    like mirrors at the bends
    of tunnels, that withhold
    your face, but give you
    what is to come;

    like the voice at the end
    of the tunnel, that says
    'Terminus', almost
    tenderly —

Little twigs that snap
like gunshot as they
consume themselves, little
dry twigs,

little sparks, little pops, little bursts
at the smoky heart of where it
begins again, o,

tender and sunny love! what, are you gone
so far away?

Come home to me now, my
brightness. Make a small glow.
Make it to move
the heart, that has sat down
in the road

and waits for something
to turn it over ...

    The roomy heart,
    willing to be surprised.

Robyn Sarah

Heart Island

Between New York and Canada are the Thousand Islands,
each one about the right size for a house with a yard,
each one owned by a person who imagined

a life surrounded by water. Among these, Heart Island
has a castle where no one lives. It was built by
George Boldt, owner of a fancy New York hotel,

for his pretty wife, Louise. This was the Gilded Age
and the great stone stairways were as grand
as love. But Louise did not live long and the castle

was never finished. She was never caressed
by the light in the windows, did not stand
in the highest tower admiring her view. Love is

like this: a castle built for someone who will not
enjoy it. So much time spent planning the light fixtures,
the color of the carpet, while love's object is elsewhere.

Maybe Louise wanted the castle and maybe she didn't.
Either way, it stands empty, gazing out at the water:
its windows without glass, its kitchen always cold, its rooms

so bare it's hard to believe pleasure ever designed them.

— *Faith Shearin*

Crush

Chris was 13. I believed her adult. Tall, she was, composed,
the finest athlete in our school, and me the sort of girl picked last
for teams or terrors of Red Rover, afraid of contact and
expecting pain. I could not throw, I could not catch,
I could not hit the ball. I was her tennis partner, chosen, and
grateful beyond words.

                         She was calm and loose-limbed, strong.
Her face appeared to glow above the crowd.
Did I follow like a puppy, moon-face, lips a-quiver?
She did not seem to take offence.

                         Once, I sat beside her while
she bathed, rivulets of steam all down the long windows. I told her things.
She listened, sitting in that deep warm bath, she breathed.
She nodded, solemn and aware.

                       To close my eyes, I see
the curve of lashes glisten on her cheek.

Love!
How it surprised me then, how it did shake my heart. That first
of many times. This one I don't speak of. This one I let go.

Carolyn Smart

Lost Heart Highway

**Imperceptible
it withers in the world
this flower-like human heart.**
— Ono No Komachi, 9th Century, Japan

Driving alone/with you
through Nebraska,
hot, dusty, dry, after the boulders of Colorado,
the blue hills of New Mexico.

When love goes,
the heart's petals fall
she loves me, he loves me not
On the second floor of the deserted cabin,
the whores' ghosts gather
for one last dance,
red petticoats twirling, tumbling,
hair and shawls askew.
They sing us to sleep and to wakefulness
with siren songs of life,
offer moist kisses, bare breasts sweet with perfume.
They carry their feather beds on their backs,
they are made of feathers,
maids of feathers,
soft, free-floating,
flying away in the morning sun,
sun-flowers staring into the gaze of the world

they have lost and found their hearts so many times,
given them away in pieces,
now they are almost at peace.

Driving with you/alone through the heart of the country
into the ghost town of love.

⌣ *Ellen S. Jaffe*

Match

You live in a house of sound and you live
with a ghost. The one who stole your heart
also lives in your heart so you cut it out
with a carving knife and send it flying.
You say sometimes you wake and wait
for the god of loneliness to leave you alone.
I say our city is small and teeming
with ghosts and there are no seasons
for hiding. So we let go of the ones
who called us by our names. We make
ourselves new names by tracing letters
in a sand tray with sharp stones.
This is called Patience or Practicing
Solitude or The Wind Will Ruin Everything
but what does it matter let's go for beauty
every time. You say the price we pay for love
is loss. I say the price we pay for love
is love. You say sometimes you've nothing
save your hand in the glove and the glove
against wind and you're jabbing at the sky now
in the match of your life but the sky
never fights back so you praise it.

Brynn Saito

Assiniboine

Deep summer nights and you, far off, quiet in the dawn.
That last morning the mute swans were on the river and I was unclean.
I placed hot stones in water as you told me of the old people
beside the slow current singing. If I look hard enough I believe
I can see the swans slide past on that long river going toward the lake.
It took many stones, you weaving grouse feathers in your hair, and laughing.
Do you remember the swans? The birds whose wings were song?
Your mother told you they were ghost birds. *But she was crazy*, you said
And then the city and you lost again the in the bars, the empty rooms.
It was the time when one of my last lives was changing.
I looked hard, but there was no finding you.
I turned all the way around then and headed west toward the grey rain.
It was a far way, that walking to the place where the sun drowns.

~ *Patrick Lane*

The Heart Falls Asleep

The heart falls asleep,
not gradually, not knowing how exactly, but all at once,
like a suddenly emptied thing, a cloth doll
tossed into a corner and left there,
accidental, helpless, a light being shut off, the
hum of trains, a man in the subway
pushing the mop in front of him for the last time
tonight, the spirit gone out of it,
the last feeling, a candle about to go out
in a pool of its own wax
that melts through at the last minute.
The heart falls asleep,
the quiet sleep of machines, of finding pitch,
of running smoothly, the sleep of economy, of
no hesitation to the sound,
not of fatigue, or forgetfulness,
or envy, just straight ahead.
The heart falls asleep.
Why not? What has to be done it does
with its eyes closed. Why bother,
the ribs hum, the body hums,
things will not hang together, even the hand turns away
unfinished, nothing comes out right
and so the heart falls asleep,
because there is too much it wants,
so much that even in its sleep it can't stay still,
it stretches, it makes a small sound, a sound
like metal fatiguing, a line being scratched on glass,
things of no order, no focus,
and then it says without knowing it
that it does not want you to be gone.

— Kim Maltman

Intermittent Rain

Rain hitting the shovel
leaned against the house,
rain hitting the edges
of the metal in tiny bites,
bloating the handle,
cracking it.
The rain quits and starts again.

There are people who go into that room in the house
where the piano is and close the door.
They play to get at that thing
on the tip of the tongue,
the thing they think of first and never say.
They would leave it out in the rain if they could.

The heart is a shovel leaning against a house somewhere
among the other forgotten tools.
The heart, it's always digging up old ground,
always wanting to give things a decent burial.

But so much stays fugitive,
inside,
where it can't be reached.

The piano is a way of practising
speech when you have no mouth.
When the heart is a shovel that would bury itself.
Still we can go up casually to a piano
and sit down and start playing
the way the rain felt in someone else's bones
a hundred years ago,
before we were born,
before we were even one cell,
when the world was clean,
when there were no hearts or people,
the way it sounded
a billion years ago, pattering
into unknown ground. Rain

hitting the shovel leaned against the house,
eating the edges of the metal.
It quits,
    and starts again.

Roo Borson

Possession is 9/10th of the Love

Dreaming about my former husband,
as one must on occasion
as if to fulfill some unwritten law
of the heart, I found him
unrecognizable. I do not know how I knew
my ex. The new man
was slovenly and stout, with black
hair and a wicked goatee.
Though I harbour no hostility, no current grudges,
I wonder at the transformation in the unconscious.
Awake I remember how he always shone:
·an Aryan god, golden, like white wine
when the hue's almost green
as in the recalling of the vine by a crystal decanter
through the furtive light in the libation

before and after it is·
                    drunk.

— *Mary di Michele*

Heart

The heart can't sever its attachments, no matter how many sutras it hears, how many Tibetan prayer flags conversing with the wind. It continues to adore country folk and their tasks, unearthing potatoes dropped into a tin bucket (how the heart loves that thud), witching a well (how it leaps when the wand dips), leaning into the cow's flank to keep warm, hands pulling the teats with the heart's own rhythm. Like the brain, the heart knows detachment but also ardour. It has more horse-sense and gumption; its memory is lesser and more selective. It's an expert in eschatology: the farewell kiss on a mother's eyelids, the final sigh of an old dog who couldn't get up, sunlight trapped in a house with boarded-up windows. Half of what lived there the heart thought would kill you. Half of what lived there the heart thought would make you happy. Each of its four chambers has a different postal code, a different key, a different phone ringing through the night. In all cases it's the old-fashioned type with a circular dial, a heavy receiver. If you were to answer, to say hello, you'd hear the only words the heart cares to utter, o love, o love, o love.

Lorna Crozier

That empty house, your heart

open as a house with all its doors ajar, hot
July night, a fan in the room
across the hall, earlier a few blinds rattled
but now there's no breeze
and even in the dark the heat builds

its own house — architect, carpenter — all
the trades under its belt — in your bed,
hair lifted, bare neck on cotton pillow slip, sheetless —
heat leads you, solders you — you are a fixture
heat incorporates like an awkward tub

enclosing you in a brocade drop-cloth
while it lifts walls, vaporizes ceilings, strips veins —
heart surgeon, saws studs apart, spreads
the frame with its fingers, slows its pulsing —
then brings in trees, a city park with swings,

cinnamon rolls with brown sugar and raisins,
the ancestor who gave you knock-knees, and plaster
like a baby's skin, olive and rose — the clink of milk
bottles on the door step, throats of cream, and
a screen door by sweet peas — heat tiles the past

in a plush mosaic, turns the tap on full bore —
you're in an ocean, swimming with whales,
doors angled like fins, hall limpid with jelly-fish
in spiralling constellations — fan futile, heat's
vast and naked and is gathering you in its wave

⌐, *Jane Munro*

Buoy

Dark steering of love along the curve
and surge

his barbed tongue on the salt of her skin   her red cone
heart tipping like a buoy in the breach of water

warm-blooded float on the open sea
bobs so lightly he can cup it in his hand

tilt it to the current of his choosing
swift and deep.

How to secure a heart
with a knotted rope
of unintended promise?

She gauges the distance
she thought palpable

her hips under his

wave of breath
that follows

now compressed to
dead weight and
a crooked line of air.

Carol Lipszyc

Heart

Heart, let us this once reason together.
Thou art a child no longer. Only think
What sport the neighbors have from us, not without cause.
These nightly sulks, these clamorous demonstrations!
Already they tell of thee a famous story.
An antique, balding spectacle such as thou art,
Affecting still that childish, engaging stammer
With all the seedy innocence of an overripe pomegranate!
Henceforth, let us conduct ourselves more becomingly!

And still I hear thee, beating thy little fist
Against the walls. My dear, have I not led thee,
Dawn after streaky dawn, besotted, home?
And still these threats to have off as before?
From thee, who wouldst lose thyself in the next street?
Go then, O my inseparable, this once more.
Afterwards we will take thought for our good name.

— *Donald Justice*

Puzzle

The heart has its reasons which reason knows not.
— Blaise Pascal

Lately my sister's heart refuses the simple life,
    a plot of land, a few chickens, a goat.
It has become difficult and complicated and rampages
through the backstreets of beach towns, tossing beer cans into ditches.

She has come to believe her heart is a seventeen-year-old boy
in a souped-up truck, engine revving, wheels spitting gravel.
It shifts gears without warning, trashes the house,
then begs forgiveness.

These days my sister asks for little,
just that her heart behave like other sensible hearts —
no antics or sulking, no fibrillation.
Is a single day of steady drumbeats too much to ask?

When she woke this morning her heart was already up
to its old flip-flopping tricks. Sometimes it gets stuck,
an LP skipping at the end. Other times it drives her
to the edge of the breakwater or back to bed.

And where did they go, those heart-strong days
    when we played house
beneath the cedar's swooping branches.
Swept and swept but our dirt floor never came clean.

She bends over the picnic table, snaps another blue tile into place.
Can a heart tire of being a heart?
Can a thousand interlocking pieces make up a sky?

Patricia Young

Interlocutor

There's a heart in my right side that
answers the other one,
obsessed with its nullity nullity;
pokes till the sleeper
flutters up. But
I tell you it's my right heart that flies
in the face of death, it
curses chews on crackers snaps its knuckles
whistles Tea for Two and taps out
the Mourner's Kaddish in soft shoe.
The other one nods, reassuring itself.
This is recorded
by a breath that has no room.
My heart struggles with my heart,
and between them
I am the bone.

— *Roger Greenwald*

Heart to Heart

It's neither red
nor sweet.
It doesn't melt
or turn over,
break or harden,
so it can't feel
pain,
yearning,
regret.

It doesn't have
a tip to spin on,
it isn't even
shapely —
just a thick clutch
of muscle,
lopsided,
mute. Still,
I feel it inside
its cage sounding
a dull tattoo:
I want, I want —

but I can't open it:
there's no key.
I can't wear it
on my sleeve,
or tell you from
the bottom of it
how I feel. Here,
it's all yours, now —
but you'll have
to take me,
too.

— **Rita Dove**

Turn

after Whitman

I wear myself inside
out. If you miss

me, do not look now
under your boot soles.

I am not yet plotted.
I keep my heart still

where it belongs:
here in my mouth.

— *Miriam N. Kotzin*

Slumbering Woman

See this woman who dons injury
like a vintage mink stole,
weathered tail wrapped
around her shoulders   across her chest.

She lives where tenderness follows
the bruising word   where tell-tale wounds leave
an indelible print.

Sleeps where night is mercenary -
regrets and remorse
their double henchmen.

Odd, how in the dark, regrets find refuge —
come daylight they trail her in shadow steps.

Should her heart open its trap door
tap like a child in the play-penned hour
she will answer -

If only I could, I would...

her refrain grazing
her slumbering heart.

Carol Lipszyc

Whittled Heart

Down to a core
I whittled my heart.

Its outer bows
quickly given

with little thought
of what comes next —

for scarves,
and shin guards,

cereal bowls,
and protractors —

lamp light
and all that bends

'its arms
toward others.

But the inner bows
were offered

more slowly
as leaves

unfurled,
green reminders,

that finally,
decades old

fell off us,
fell away.

— *Beverly Ellenbogen*

Chamber

Opening a chamber
of his heart

he shovels in something
that will at least burn,

childhood furniture —
desk top, book end,

something drier
than all his love,

a deluge
down the hatch.

No hands to pass it back,
no one to lean and whisper to.

Just rooms getting cleaner,
a courage of tidying.

He needs to toss in
something daily now —

chair frame, hamper,
board game.

Night peers into
this engine of his heart,

does it beat with industry,
forcing hours down the track?

He shovels in the past,
all that grins with pain

laptop screen light,
dawn birds nattering.

Heave it all in and watch,
without me.

⌐ *Beverly Ellenbogen*

The Heart As Lamb

The heart is a novice.

It has seen the wolf,
it knows the scent;
yet it continues bleating certitude,
grazing on the splendid world
as if wolves did not exist.

The mouth, however,
is a different breed;
panic squirms inside it
like a trap-bitten beast.

While the mouth prays for certainty,
the heart eyes the wolf
and eats
and lives.

Eva Tihanyi

Night in the Arms
of the Two-Hearted Lover

(unidentified woman discovered
March 26, 1986 near San Antonio, Texas)

The night is full of wolves, dear,
and the angels are restless.

Here the dark slit of road unravels
east of the San Antonio line

and my arms are a cavalry of precision
wrapped hard around your waistband.

Between my thighs, your engine vibrates
dusk across the sky of exposed skin

and I roll my tongue around yours
because this is what you want.

We rest cheeks against the sides of a farmhouse
like a giant beast we once remembered.

Here we pray to the gods of transformation,
hunters with metal and sacrifice

and you say you know the evil
of magic woven 'round hoed earth.

Beneath your startled hands
you know the pulse of the shadows.

In the distance, the dark pull
of a train heading north across the flats

and we both wail, thrashing
against the passage.

Here the night wings flit close
to blood spilled out on Texas sand

and we hold open our palms
because there's still a heart

beating in the night, dear.

Aimée Baker

Raimon De Roussillon

This *trobador*, this Guillem de Cabestany
so loved his *domna* as to include in his *vers*
more detail than convention required. One could
without excessive cerebration guess
who the woman was, as Raimon, her husband, did.
The sweet love song in his ears was bitter, harsh,
in other words, a *trobar brau*, to which
he wanted to respond in a brutal way
beyond mere versification. Never mind
the pen; the sword has its uses too. He killed
the presumptuous and also indiscreet
Guillem. But that was not yet a work of art.
He cut out the fucker's heart, brought it back to the *castel*
and directed his cook to do whatever it took
to make it at least palatable or, better,
tasty. (The consequences of failure were dire.)
So a couple of onions, just under a pound of carrots,
and oranges, one squeezed for the juice and the other
cut into small sections. With butter and onions
in eight wedges, he browned in a cocotte
(which is, in one sense, a prostitute, but also
a small baking dish that respectable women use)
the heart he'd been given. Then the carrots, white wine,
salt, pepper, the orange juice and the sections,
he cooked for a couple of hours over low heat,
and sprinkled them with chopped cilantro — *voilà,*
prêt à servir.

        It was Seremonda's dinner:
she ate it with pleasure, even gusto, and asked
what it was. He told her: Guillem's heart
that he had declared in his well-known poem was hers.
She killed herself that night — not unexpected,
a part of the plan, in fact.

                              Poetic justice?
Doesn't require words, is better without them.

⁓ **David R. Slavitt**

My Heart

I'd like to give my heart away as a present
It always only brings me sadness anyway

I would like to sew it to a cripple's crutch
Under his arm it would be a soft pillow

They could cut my heart in two, to make
Red shoes for a little beggar girl

Or I'd give it to her grieving mother
It may be meat enough for one dinner

   Ernő Szép
     Translated by Eva M. Thury

The Tell-Tale Heart

Sex is a box built by Poe.
Long before Freud he knew

to gauge the walls' sliding
in on
each other just so, the breathing
space for potential

escape growing smaller
at an unfixed but
observable rate. He knew just how
loose to tie bonds

around wrists and ankles
to make struggle
more desperate, the head jerked firmly
in place to better

watch the pendulum swing
lower,
the sharp edge of fate
shining brightly like intent.

Here indecision is duped.
What is hidden by uneasy flesh
is brutally cut free
by the hypnotic stroke of the blade.

Here guilt is a pawn,
and love, that dream of the self,
falls away like meat from the bone.
What must be will be:

listen to the cries of the heart
bite their way out.

⟿ *John Barton*

When We Lie

When we lie with our bodies
mapped like an instinct to one another
does it bereave you to know?
The knife-thrust — yes love — is aimed
just below your heart. And upwards
into the hilly regions where wild
feelings still roam untrammelled
by thought and property.

Where 'fuck' is a holy word and the gullible
beast stares wide-eyed at a world
of compulsion, stamping like a child
in a glass womb.

So remember the pain, the salt-edge
meeting place (just below the heart),
the central fact rubbed in again and again and again:
This is the essential geography,
the mauve outline of a lamb caught high in the gorse,
its belly ripped from breast to crotch,
tongue lolling.
The damage — don't forget — was done when you pulled out
the knife and love came gushing
till not even a fist
could hold it back.

— *Michael Mirolla*

heart

whether to take an axe to this
loose shutter and its insistent clattering,

or not; to draw, perhaps, the hammer back
and drive the bolt into its

place. whether to cleave.   there is,

no doubt, a force in this — the kind of thing
that bursts barrels and topples

stacks of whatever might not be
nailed tightly down.

      whether to simply make our way

over to the door and be done
with it.   to spread our arms; to brace

our shoulders against the hard angle
of the frame. to just make do

right there, standing at the threshold of:

⸺ *Matt Robinson*

Mongrel Heart

Up the dog bounds to the window, baying
    like a basset his doleful, tearing sounds
        from the belly, as if mourning a dead king,

and now he's howling like a beagle — yips, brays,
    gagging growls — and scratching the sill paintless,
        that's how much he's missed you, the two of you,

both of you, mother and daughter, my wife
    and child. All week he's curled at my feet,
        warming himself and me watching more TV,

or wandered the lonely rooms, my dog shadow,
    who like a poodle now hops, amped-up windup
        maniac yo-yo with matted curls and snot nose

smearing the panes, having heard another car
    like yours taking its grinding turn down
        our block, or a school bus, or bird-squawk,

that's how much he's missed you, good dog,
    companion dog, dog-of-all-types, most excellent dog
        I told you once and for all we should never get.

— *David Baker*

Bluebird

there's a bluebird in my heart that
wants to get out
but I'm too tough for him,
I say, stay in there, I'm not going
to let anybody see
you.
there's a bluebird in my heart that
wants to get out
but I pour whiskey on him and inhale
cigarette smoke
and the whores and the bartenders
and the grocery clerks
never know that
he's
in there.

there's a bluebird in my heart that
wants to get out
but I'm too tough for him,
I say,
stay down, do you want to mess
me up?
you want to screw up the
works?
you want to blow my book sales in
Europe?
there's a bluebird in my heart that
wants to get out
but I'm too clever, I only let him out
at night sometimes
when everybody's asleep.
I say, I know that you're there,
so don't be
sad.
then I put him back,
but he's singing a little
in there, I haven't quite let him
die

and we sleep together like
that
with our
secret pact
and it's nice enough to
make a man
weep, but I don't
weep, do
you?

━ *Charles Bukowski*

Two Countries

1.

"Two Women, One Heart."
I remember hearing the song on the radio
on my way across the loping black roads of Kentucky
to visit Matt Walker. With his beard full,
he looked twice his age. Or perhaps I thought this
because he seemed grown-up,
the owner of a collision repair shop,
his last name painted in crooked letters on a front-lawn sign.
Over coffee at the local diner,
he confessed to loving two women,
the one he was dating, dark-haired, half American Indian,
and the one he would soon see in Texas,
hair the color of butter and legs toned
from the three-times-a-week aerobics class she taught.
"Christine," he said. "Rhymes with dream."
It didn't, but I understood.
Our hearts were large and greedy,
and we were young enough to think
the world couldn't fill them.

2.

Coming back to Guatemala,
I feel like a snake trying to find its old skin.
It fit once, perfectly,
or so I thought, dreaming in Spanish,
berating the bus drivers' *ayudantes*
with native indignation.
I learned the form 'vos,'
sang ranchera songs with the radio,
danced salsa, swinging my hips.
A friend said, "You're more *Guatemalteco* than gringo."
I raised a bottle of Gallo to the flattery I believed.

A tourist now, I slither around streets
I used to know the cracks of,
find myself at the ends of strange cul-de-sacs.
From a church, I hear the loud prayers of Evangelicals,
asking to be re-born.
I retreat to my room, drink tepid cans of Gallo
and imagine conversations with people
I used to see every day in the park.

3.

The children I knew in Santa Cruz Verapaz have grown up;
some work sorting asparagus in the factory on the highway,
others have gone to try their luck in the capital.
Several who have found jobs in town
wave to me from doorways where their parents used to stand
as I raced by on my Shimano;
it was red and had a high seat,
and I rode it over trails cut like signatures into mountains.
One morning I changed a tire beside a creek,
dipping the tube into cold water
to see where it leaked.
The air bubbled like breath.

When, after I'd been in Guatemala for three years,
my students convinced me to sing "The Star-Spangled Banner,"
I surprised myself: I cried.
I hadn't thought of what I was missing.
Baseball games, Politics and Prose, snow;
my mother, father, sister — my cat and car.
Two countries, one heart.

4.

I loved your smell
and how your voice could sound
like the subway, Broadway, Central Park.
You had trouble sleeping
and I staggered with you into unrestful mornings,
cab drivers as reckless and industrious at dawn
as they'd been at midnight.
A city with insomnia.
A woman of the dreams I would have dreamed
had I been able.

No matter the hiss of trucks sweeping Amsterdam
of the remnants of another weekend;
no matter the annoyed car horns
and busses grumbling.
This morning your room is warm and the sunlight soft,
and we can even whisper and be heard
when stoplights hold the traffic
with their bloodshot eyes.

5.

Matt Walker had to sell his shop.
The super dealer in the next town sucked up his work.
One of its eight painters now, he is married, two kids,
I think, although perhaps I only want to believe this.
We've lost touch. I can only picture him
as I am — traveled and ready to rest
in the solace the heart offers
when it is full enough.

⌐ *Mark Brazaitis*

Noble Matter

You can still hear it beating
against your chest.
So many, many years exposed
to the violence of the light
at noon. Almost bitter,
almost sweet. Only passion steals it
from death, keeps it from being
a riddled pot
through which the wind whistles.
Or worse, a sticky thing, spongy,
inert. The heart,
noble matter.

— *Eugénio de Andrade*
  Translated by Alexis Levitin

Body Part

I offer you the same old gift again:
This ancient shriveled organ of my flesh
That we have used since who remembers when?

It's shoddy now, but it was strong and fresh
When we were young. You held it in your hand
And felt its pulse when we had seed to thresh.

It throbbed for you and needed no command
To flame and ache when it was called upon
To do its duty, dilate and expand

To fill the evening or the breaking dawn,
The morn or afternoon with the lover's art ...,
So many years have passed now and have gone

To seed, so many organs have come apart —
Still, I offer you this same old heart.

— *Lewis Turco*

Credits for Previous Publications

"The Heart is Improvisational," by Carol Lipszyc. Published in *the lonely crowd, spring, The Lonely Press*, 2016. Reprinted with permission of the publisher.

"Average Life," by Susan Glickman. Published in *The Smooth Yarrow* by Signal Editions of Vehicle Press, 2012. Reprinted with permission of the author.

"Cardiognosis," (excerpt) by David Baker. Published in *Midwest Eclogue* by W.W. Norton & Company, Inc., 2007. Reprinted with permission of the publisher.

"Heart," by Kenneth Sherman. Published in *Exile Literary Quarterly* 2011 (vol. 35, no. 1). Reprinted with permission of the author.

"L27011945" (from *Heart Archives*) by Sue Rose. First published in her chapbook, *Heart Archives* by Hercules Editions, 2014. Reprinted in *The Cost of Keys* by Cinnamon Press, 2014. Reprinted here with permission of the author.

"Heart Valve," by Elizabeth Arnold. Published in *Life* by Flood Editions, 2014. Copyright © 2014 by Elizabeth Arnold. Reprinted with permission of the publisher.

"Aviary," by Miriam N. Kotzin. First published in *Boulevard* Vol. 30 (Fall 2015). Reprinted in her collection, *Debris Field*, David Robert Books, 2017. Reprinted here with permission of the author.

"Flow Dynamics," by Elizabeth Arnold. Published in *Life* by Flood Editions, 2014. Copyright © 2014 by Elizabeth Arnold. Reprinted with permission of the publisher.

"Donor," by Tamar Yoseloff. Published in *Sweetheart* by Slow Dancer Books, 1998. Reprinted with permission of the author.

"Transplanted," by Lorna Crozier. Published in *Small Mechanics* by McLelland & Stewart, 2011. Copyright © 2011 by Lorna Crozier. Reprinted with permission of McLelland & Stewart, a division of Random House of Canada Limited, a Penguin Random House Company.

"An Unabridged History of the Heart," by Eva Tihanyi. Published in *Wresting the Grace of the World* by Black Moss Press, 2005. Reprinted with permission of the author.

"Love," by Faith Shearin. Published in *The Owl Question* by Utah State University Press, 2002. Reprinted with permission of the publisher.

"Blue Bird," by Elizabeth Cohen. Published in *Mother Love* by Keshet Press, 2007. Reprinted in *Bird Light* by St. Julian Press 2016. Reprinted here with permission of the author.

"When They Are Asleep In Their Nimbus Of Flame," by Susan Glickman. Published in *Running in Prospect Cemetery: New and Selected Poems* by Signal Editions of Vehicle Press, 2004. Reprinted with permission of the author.

"Love Poem for My Daughter," by Marilyn Bowering. First published in *The Alchemy of Happiness* by Beach Holme Publishing. Copyright © 2002 by Marilyn Bowering. Reprinted here with permission of Dundurn Press Limited.

"Love," by Jerry Mirskin. Published in *Saranac Review*, Issue 7 (2011). Reprinted with permission of the author.

"Loop," by Kate Marshall Flaherty. Published in *Stone Soup* by Quattro Books, 2015. Reprinted with permission of the author.

"B02031929," (from *Heart Archives*) by Sue Rose. First published in her chapbook, *Heart Archives* by Hercules Editions, 2014. Reprinted in *The Cost of Keys* by Cinnamon Press, 2014. Reprinted here with permission of the author.

"Mud in Heaven," by Doug Ramspeck. First published in *Rhino* (2010):78. Reprinted in his collection, *Possum Nocturne* as "Raising the Dust," by NorthShore Press, 2010. Reprinted here with permission of the publisher.

"If My Father Had Written Poems," by Ellen S. Jaffe. First published in *Voices Israel* 2013. Reprinted in her collection, *Skinny-Dipping with the Muse,* Guernica Editions, 2014. Reprinted here with permission of the author.

"Flocking," by Ellen S. Jaffe. First published in her chapbook, *Twelve Moons and Six More Poems,* Pinking Shears Publications, 2010. Reprinted in *Skinny-Dipping With the Muse,* Guernica Editions, 2014. Reprinted here with permission of the author.

"A Birthday Poem," by Daniel Boland. Published in *Detours* by Stone Flower Press, 2014. Reprinted with permission of the author.

"Olympia Marblewing Butterfly," by David Reibetanz. Published in *Fiddlehead,* Edition No. 236, Summer 2008. Reprinted with permission of the author.

"Theoretical Chest," by Doug Ramspeck. First published in EPOCH 58.2 (2009):150. Reprinted in his collection, *Mechanical Fireflies* by Barrow Street Press, 2011. Reprinted here with permission of the author.

"Nirvana," by John Barton. Published in *West of Darkness: Emily Carr, A Self-Portrait* by Dundurn Press Limited, 1999. Reprinted with permission of the publisher.

"Print," by M. Travis Lane. First published in *The Moosehead Review* (No 8 1984). Reprinted in her collection, *Reckonings, poems 1978-1985* by Goose Lane, 1988. Reprinted here with permission of the author.

"Lo, and Behold" by Elizabeth Cohen. First published online by *Exquisite Corpse,* 2008. Reprinted in her collection, *Bird Light* by St. Julian Press, 2016. Reprinted here with permission of the author.

"Poem on Good Friday," by Daniel Boland. Published in *Detours* by Stone Flower Press, 2014. Reprinted with permission of the author.

"L'avalasse," by Jack B. Bedell. Published in *Come Rain, Come Shine* by Texas Review Press, 2006. Reprinted with permission of the author.

"Fisherman," by Sheryl St. Germain. First published in *How Heavy the Breath of God* by the University of North Texas Press, 1994. Reprinted in *Let It Be a Dark Roux: New and Selected Poems* by Autumn House Press, 2007. Reprinted here with permission of the author.

"Temple," by Kate Marshall Flaherty. Published in *Stone Soup* by Quattro Books, 2015. Reprinted with permission of the author.

"Open Night," by David Reibetanz. Published in *Black Suede Cave* by Guernica Editions, 2013. Reprinted with permission of the publisher.

"Fiesole," by Jerry Mirskin. First published in *Ascent*. Reprinted in his collection, *Picture a Gate Hanging Open and Let that Gate be the Sun* by Mammoth Books Press, 2002. Reprinted here with permission of the author.

"Venice," by Jerry Mirskin. Published in *In Flagrante Delicto* by Mammoth Books, 2008. Reprinted with permission of the author.

"The Human Heart," by Campbell McGrath. Published in *Pax Atomica* by Ecco Press, a publishing imprint of Harper Collins Publishers, 2004. Reprinted with permission of Harper Collins Publishers.

"The Inhabited Heart," by Eugénio de Andrade, translation by Alexis Levitin. Published in *Forbidden Words: Selected Poetry of Eugénio de Andrade* by New Directions Publishing Corp, 2003. Copyright © 1995 by Eugénio de Andrade; translation 1995, 2003 by Alexis Levitin. Reprinted with permission of New Directions Publishing Corp.

"My Heart Hears You Dreaming," by Eva Tihanyi. First published in *Wresting the Grace of the World* by Black Moss Press, 2005. Reprinted in *Flying Underwater: Poems New and Selected* by Inanna Publications, 2012. Reprinted here with permission of the author.

"Let Your Heart," by Eva Tihanyi. Published in *In the Key of Red* by Inanna Publications, 2010. Reprinted with permission of the author.

"Naked Hearts," by John Barton. Published in *For the Boy with the Eyes of the Virgin: Selected Poems* by Nightwood Editions, 2012, www.nightwoodeditions.com. Reprinted with permission of the publisher.

"The Request," by Michael Carrino. First published in *Z-Miscellaneous*, 1988. Reprinted in his collection, *Some Rescues*, by New Poet Series, 1994. Reprinted here with permission of the author.

"Valentine" and "We Kissed As Lovers Under Widowed Light," by Charles Fort. Both poems were published in *We Did Not Fear the Father, New and Selected Poems* by Red Hen Press, 2012. Reprinted with permission of the publisher.

"The Hearts," by Malca Litovitz. Published in *First Day* by Guernica, 2008. Reprinted with permission of the publisher.

"In the Garden," by Michael Carrino. First published in *The Glen Falls Review*, 1986. Reprinted in his collection, *Some Rescues,* by New Poet Series, 1994. Reprinted here with permission of the author.

"Scratch," by Robyn Sarah. First published in *Becoming Light* by Cormorant, 1987. Reprinted in *The Touchstone: Poems New and Selected* by Anansi, 1992. Reprinted here with permission of the author.

"Heart Island," by Faith Shearin. Published in *Poetry East #69*. Reprinted with permission of the author.

"Lost Heart Highway," by Ellen S. Jaffe. First published in her chapbook, *Twelve Moons and Six More Poems,* Pinking Shears Publications, 2010. Reprinted in *Skinny-Dipping With the Muse*, Guernica Editions, 2014. Reprinted here with permission of the author. "Lost Heart Highway" was inspired by Anne Mandlsohn's art show "Lost Heart Highway," which combined the artist's original prints, paintings, and photographs with Japanese poetry; the poem by Ono No Komachi, from this exhibit, is used with permission of the artist.

"Match," by Brynn Saito. First published in *Ninth Letter*'s Spring/Summer Issue, Vol. 9, No. 1. Renamed "Spring, San Francisco," it was reprinted in *The Palace of Contemplating Departure*, by Red Hen Press, 2013. Reprinted here with permission of the publisher.

"Assiniboine," by Patrick Lane. Published in *Washita* by Harbour Publishing, 2014. Reprinted with permission of the publisher.

"The Heart Falls Asleep," by Kim Maltman. Published in *The Transparence of November/Snow* by Roo Borson and Kim Maltman, by Quarry Press, 1985. Reprinted with permission of the author.

"Intermittent Rain," by Roo Borson. First published in *Intent, Or the Weight of the World* by McClelland & Stewart, 1989. Reprinted in *Night*

Walk: Selected Poems, by Oxford University Press, 1994. Reprinted here with permission of the author.

"Possession is 9/10th of the Love," by Mary di Michele. Published in *Luminous Emergencies* by McClelland & Stewart, 1990. Reprinted with permission of the author.

"Heart," by Lorna Crozier. First published in *Small Mechanics* by McClelland & Stewart, 2011. Reprinted in *The Book of Marvels: A Compendium of Everyday Things*, 2013 by Greystone Books Ltd. Reprinted here with permission of Greystone Books.

"That empty house, your heart," by Jane Munro. Published in *Active Pass* by Pedlar Press, 2010. Copyright © 2010 by Jane Munro. Reprinted with permission of the author.

"Buoy," by Carol Lipszyc. Published in *Per Contra*, Issue 40 summer-2016, Poetry. Reprinted with permission of the publisher.

"Heart," by Donald Justice. Published in *Collected Poems* by Penguin Random House, 2004. Copyright © 2004 by Donald Justice. Reprinted with permission of Alfred A. Knopf, an imprint of the Knopf Doubleday Publishing Group, a division of Penguin Random House LLC.

"Puzzle," by Patricia Young. First published in *Freefall Magazine*, Volume XXIV Number 2. Reprinted in her collection, *Short Takes on the Apocalypse* by Biblioasis, 2016. Reprinted here with permission of Biblioasis.

"Interlocutor," by Roger Greenwald. Published in *Slow Mountain Train* by Tiger Bark Press. © 2015 by Roger Greenwald. Reprinted with permission of the author.

"Heart to Heart," by Rita Dove. Published in *American Smooth* by W.W. Norton & Company, Copyright ©2004 by Rita Dove. Reprinted with permission of the author.

"Turn," by Miriam N. Kotzin. Published in *Weights & Measures* by Star Cloud Press, 2009. Reprinted with permission of the author.

"The Heart as Lamb," by Eva Tihanyi. First published in *Prophecies Near the Speed of Light* by Thistledown Press, 1984. Reprinted in *Flying*

Underwater: Poems New and Selected by Inanna Publicatons, 2012. Reprinted here with permission of the author.

"Night in the Arms of the Two-Hearted Lover," by Aimée Baker. Published in *The Pinch*, Spring 2015 (35.1). Copyright © 2015 by Aimée Baker. Reprinted with permission of the publisher.

"Raimon De Roussillon," by David Slavitt. Published in *Civil Wars* by Louisiana State University Press, 2013. Reprinted with permission of the publisher.

"My Heart," by Ernő Szép. Translation of "Szívem" by Eva Thury. First published in *Jó szó. (Versek. 1922–1928)* by Singer és Wolfer in Budapest in 1929. Copyright © (1929) by Ernő Szép. Translation © (1999) Eva Thury. Previously published in *Per Contra* 33 (Fall 2014). Reprinted here with permission of Peter Lantos.

"Where We Lie," by Michael Mirolla. First published in *Underpass #4*, 1990. Reprinted in *Light and Time* by Guernica Editions, 2010. Reprinted here with permission of the author.

"Mongrel Heart," by David Baker. Published in *The Southeast Review*, Vol 23, No. 2, 2005. Reprinted with permission of the author.

"Bluebird," by Charles Bukowski. Published in *Last Night of the Earth Poems* by Harper Collins Publishers, 1992. Reprinted with permission of the publisher.

"Two Countries," by Mark Brazaitis. Published in *The Notre Dame Review* (Issue 6) Summer, 1998. Reprinted with permission of the author.

"Noble Matter," by Eugénio de Andrade, translation by Alexis Levitin. Published in *The Art of Patience* by Red Dragon Fly Press, 2013. Reprinted with permission of the publisher.

"Body Part," by Lewis Turco. Published in *Trinacria*, Issue 33, 2014. Reprinted with permission of the author.

Biographical Notes

Eugénio de Andrade (1923–2005) was, after Fernando Pessoa, the best known Portuguese poet of the 20th century. He won all of Portugal's literary awards, as well as the prestigious Prix Jean Malrieu from France. His work has appeared in well over twenty languages. In North America, eleven volumes of his work have appeared: *Inhabited Heart, White on White, Memory of Another River, Solar Matter, Another Name for Earth, The Shadow's Weight, The Slopes of a Gaze, Close to Speech, Dark Domain, Forbidden Words: Selected Poetry of Eugénio de Andrade,* and *The Art of Patience.*

Winner of an Amy Lowell travel grant, a Whiting award, and a Bunting fellowship, **Elizabeth Arnold** has published three books of poetry, *The Reef, Civilization,* and *Effacement.* She is on the MFA faculty of University of Maryland and lives outside Washington, D.C.

Aimée Baker is the author of *Doe,* winner of the Akron Prize and forthcoming from the University of Akron Press. She received her MFA from Arizona State University and works as an adjunct lecturer. Her poetry, fiction, and creative nonfiction have appeared in journals such as *The Southern Review, The Massachusetts Review, Gulf Coast,* and *Black Warrior Review.*

David Baker is author of sixteen books of poetry and prose. His latest works of poetry are *Scavenger Loop* (2015, W.W. Norton) and *Never-Ending Birds* (W.W. Norton), which was awarded the Theodore Roethke Memorial Poetry Prize in 2011. *Show Me Your Environment: Essays on Poetry, Poets, and Poems* appeared in 2014 from the University of Michigan. He teaches at Denison University and is Poetry Editor of *The Kenyon Review.*

John Barton's ten books of poetry and six chapbooks include: *For the Boy with the Eyes of the Virgin: Selected Poems* (Nightwood, 2012) and *Balletomane: The Program Notes of Lincoln Kirstein* (JackPine, 2012). He lives in Victoria, B.C., where he edits *The Malahat Review.*

Jack B. Bedell is Professor of English and coordinator of the programs in Creative Writing at Southeastern Louisiana University, where he also serves as editor of *Louisiana Literature* and director of Louisiana Literature Press. His most recent books are *Bone-Hollow, True: New & Selected Poems, Call and Response*, and *Come Rain, Come Shine*, all with Texas Review Press.

Daniel Boland has published two poetry collections. *Detours* was published in 2014 and *Toward the Chrysalis* was published in 2005 (Stone Flower Press). His poems have appeared in a variety of magazines including *The Antigonish Review, Saranac Review, and The Prairie Journal*. He lives in Ottawa with his wife Rosie and their daughter Angela.

Roo Borson's work has received the Griffin Poetry Prize and the Governor General's Award. Her most recent books of poetry are *Short Journey Upriver Toward Oishida* (2004), *Rain; road; an open boat* (2012), and *Cardinal in the Eastern White Cedar* (2017) published by McClelland & Stewart/Random House. With Kim Maltman, she writes under the pen name Baziju, whose first book, *Box Kite*, was published in 2016 by House of Anansi Press. She lives in Toronto.

Marilyn Bowering is a Canadian writer who has received many awards for poetry including the Pat Lowther Award, the Dorothy Livesay Prize and several National Magazine awards. Her work has twice been nominated for the Governor General's Prize. She was also a Fulbright Scholar at NYU. Recognition for Marilyn Bowering's fiction includes the Ethel Wilson Prize, designation of Notable Book by the New York Times, and short-listing for the world-wide Orange Prize. Her most recent works are the poetry book, *Threshold*, the novel, *What It Takes To Be Human*, and the libretto for Gavin Bryars' opera, *Marilyn Forever*.

Mark Brazaitis is the author of seven books, including *The River of Lost Voices: Stories from Guatemala*, winner of the 1998 Iowa Short Fiction Award, *The Incurables: Stories*, winner of the 2012 Richard Sullivan Prize and the 2013 Devil's Kitchen Reading Award in Prose, and *Julia & Rodrigo*, winner of the 2012 Gival Press Novel Award. His book of poems, *The Other Language*, won the 2008 ABZ First Book Poetry Contest.

An esteemed and often imitated writer of poetry and prose, the late **Charles Bukowski** (1920-1994) published forty-five books of poetry and prose, including *Pulp* (Black Sparrow, 1994), *Screams from the Balcony: Selected Letters 1960-1970* (1993), and *The Last Night of the Earth Poems* (1992). He died of leukemia in San Pedro on March 9, 1994.

Michael Carrino holds an M.F.A. in Writing from Vermont College of Fine Arts. He was an English lecturer at the State University College at Plattsburgh, New York, where he was a co-founder and poetry editor of the *Saranac Review*. Since his retirement, he has continued his involvement with the *Saranac Review* as an associate editor of poetry. He has had six books of poetry published, including *By Available Light New and Selected Poems* (Guernica Editions, 2012) and *Always Close, Forever Careless* (Kelsey Books, 2016).

Elizabeth Cohen holds an M.F.A. from Columbia University and is a professor of English at SUNY Plattsburgh. She is the author of the memoir, *The Family on Beartown Road*, co-author of the biography, *The Scalpel and the Silver Bear,* and the author of a book of a prose, *The Hypothetical Girl*, short stories about love in our time. Author of five books of poetry, her most recent collections include *Bird Light* (Saint Julian Press, 2016), and *What The Trees Said* (Split Oak Press, 2013). She lives in Plattsburgh, NY, with her daughter Ava.

Lorna Crozier has received many awards, including the Governor General's and B.C.'s Lieutenant's Governor's Award for Lifetime Achievement, as well as three honorary doctorates. An Officer of the Order of Canada, she has published 16 books of poetry. Her latest, *The Wrong Cat*, was the winner of two national awards for best book of poetry of 2015. Recent books include T*he Book of Marvels: A Compendium of Everyday Things,* and a memoir, *Small Beneath the Sky.* Her poems have been translated into several languages, including a book-length translation in French and another in Spanish, and she has read in every continent, except Antarctica. She lives on Vancouver Island with Patrick Lane, two turtles, many fish and two fine cats.

Rita Dove is a former U.S. Poet Laureate (1993-1995) and recipient of the 1987 Pulitzer Prize in poetry for *Thomas and Beulah*. The author of nine poetry collections, most recently *Sonata Mulattica* (2009) and *American Smooth* (2004), as well as a collection of short stories, a novel, and a play, she also edited the *Penguin Anthology of Twentieth-Century American Poetry* (2011). She has received numerous honors, among them the 1996 National Humanities Medal from President Clinton and the 2011 National Medal of Arts from President Obama. Rita Dove is Commonwealth Professor of English at the University of Virginia.

Beverly Baila Ellenbogen is a poet and psychological associate who resides in Vaughan, Ontario with her family. Her first book of poetry, *Footsteps on the Ceiling*, was published with Guernica Press in October 2010. She has also published poems in several collections including *Modern Morsels: A Selection of Short Canadian Fiction and Poetry*, McGraw-Hill Ryerson, and in journals such as *Saranac Review* and *Cordite Poetry Review*. Currently, she works at the York Region District School Board conducting assessments with children and consulting with educational staff and families.

Kate Marshall Flaherty has six books of poetry, including *Stone Soup*, published in 2015 by Quattro Books, *Reaching V*, published in 2014 with Guernica Editions. She has been published in journals such as *Descant, CV2, Freefall*, and *Grain*. She was short-listed for Nimrod's Pablo Neruda Poetry Prize, the Malahat Review Long Poem and Descant's Best Canadian Poem. Kate participated in "National Random Acts of Poetry" for three years, "poeming" people in hospitals, cafes, parks and libraries, and has traveled as far north as Cobalt to be a "Poet-in-the-schools." She lives in Toronto with her family, where she guides yoga/retreats/writing workshops and teen leadership days. Kate is now Toronto Rep. for the League of Canadian Poets. Poetry is her lifeline.

Charles Fort's books include *We Did Not Fear the Father* (New and Selected Poems) Red Hen Press 2012, *Mrs. Belladonna's Supper Club Waltz* (New and Selected Prose Poems) Backwaters Press, 2013, *The Town Clock Burning*, Carnegie Mellon University Press, and Frankenstein Was A Negro, Loganhouse Press. Fort's poems have appeared in *The Best American Poetry 2000, 2003, and 2016, Best of Prose Poem International, The Georgia Review*, and *The American Poetry Review*. Born in working class New Britain, Connecticut, he is the founder of the Wendy Fort Foundation Theater of Fine Arts. A MacDowell fellow, Fort is currently at work on *Sorrow Road*, One Hundred Villanelles, and a novel: *The Last Black Hippie in Connecticut*.

A recovering academic who once taught English and Canadian Literature at the University of Toronto, **Susan Glickman** works as a freelance editor and teaches creative writing at both Ryerson University and U of T. She is the author of six books of poetry, most recently *The Smooth Yarrow* (Montreal: Signal Editions of Véhicule Press, 2012); three novels, *Safe as Houses* (Cormorant 2015), *The Violin Lover* (2006) and *The Tale-Teller* (2012); a trilogy of children's books; and a work of literary history, *The Picturesque & The Sublime: A Poetics of the Canadian Landscape.*

Roger Greenwald attended The City College of New York and the Poetry Project workshop at St. Mark's Church In-the-Bowery, then completed graduate degrees at the University of Toronto. He has won two CBC Literary Awards (poetry and travel literature), as well as many awards for translations from Scandinavian languages. He has published two books of poems, *Connecting Flight* and *Slow Mountain Train.*

Ellen S. Jaffe grew up in New York City and moved to Canada in 1979; she lives in Hamilton, Ontario. Her books include *Skinny-Dipping with the Muse,* a poetry collection published by Guernica in 2014 (finalist for a Hamilton literary award), as well as her first collection, *Water Children,* a young-adult novel, *Feast of Lights,* and *Writing Your Way: Creating a Personal Journal.* A chapbook of her poems, translated into Finnish, was published in Helsinki and her writing has appeared in journals and anthologies. She has received grants for writing and artists-in-education from Ontario Arts Council and worked with Learning/Living Through the Arts and various community organizations.

One of the most esteemed and influential poets of the 20th century, **Donald Justice** (1925-2004) published fourteen books of poetry. Winner of the Pulitzer Prize in 1980 and the Bollinger Prize in 1991, he is recognized, in particular, for his mastery of both traditional and experimental form.

Miriam N. Kotzin is Professor of English at Drexel University where she teaches creative writing and literature. She is author of the novel, *The Real Deal* (Brick House Press 2012), a collection of flash fiction, *Just Desserts* (Star Cloud Press 2010) and five collections of poetry: *Reclaiming the Dead* (New American Press 2008), *Weights & Measures* (Star Cloud Press 2009), *Taking Stock* (Star Cloud Press 2010), *The Body's*

Bride (David Robert Books 2013) and *Debris Field* (David Robert Books 2017). Her poetry has received seven nominations for a Pushcart Prize. She is founding editor of *Per Contra* and has been a contributing editor of *Boulevard* since its inception.

Mindy Kronenberg is an award-winning poet and writer whose poetry, essays, and reviews have appeared in over 450 publications in the US and abroad. She teaches at SUNY Empire State College and offers workshops in the community through Poets & Writers and BOCES. She is the author of a poetry chapbook, *Dismantling the Playground* (Birnham Wood) and *Images of America: Miller Place* (Arcadia). In 2012, she was a panelist for the Council of Literary Magazines and Presses at the AWP conference in Chicago. She edits *Book/Mark Quarterly Review*, now in its 22nd year.

M. Travis Lane, B. A. Vassar, M.A., PhD, Cornell, has published seventeen collections of poetry. The most recent works include *The Witch of the Inner Wood: Collected Long Poems of M. Travis Lane* (Goose Lane 2016), *The Essential M. Travis Lane* (Porcupine's Quill 2016), and her 2015 collection published by Cormorant, *Crossover,* which was shortlisted for the 2015 Governor General's Award. Earlier works include *Ash Steps*, Cormorant Books, 2012. *The Book of Widows*, Frog Hollow Press, 2010, *The All Nighter's Radio,* Guernica Editions, 2010. She has won numerous honours, among them the Pat Lowther Memorial Award, the Banff Centre Bliss Carman Award, the Atlantic Poetry Prize, and the Alden Nowlan Prize for Literary Excellence. Canadian by choice, she has lived in Fredericton, New Brunswick since 1960.

Patrick Lane is one of Canada's pre-eminent poets and multi-genre writers, having won the Governor General's Award for Poetry, the Canadian Authors Association Award, the Lieutenant Governor's Award for Literary Excellence and three National Magazine Awards. Recent publications of poetry that showcase his body of work include: *The Collected Poems of Patrick Lane* (Harbour, 2011) and *Witness Selected Poems 1962-2010 (Harbour,* 2010). Writing in the memoir genre, he has published *What the Stones Remember: A Life Rediscovered* (Shambala, 2006) and *There is a Season* (McClelland and Stewart, 2004). Patrick has been a writer in residence and teacher at Concordia University in Montreal, Quebec, the University of Victoria in British Columbia, and the University of Toronto in Ontario, sharing his gifts and expertise.

Alexis Levitin has published his translations, mostly from the Portuguese, in over two hundred literary magazines, including *Partisan Review, Kenyon Review, American Poetry Review,* and *Prairie Schooner.* His forty books of translations include eleven volumes of work by Eugénio de Andrade. From Brazil, he has published Clarice Lispector's *Soulstorm* (New Directions), Astrid Cabral's *Cage* (Host Publications), and Salgado Maranhão's *Blood of the Sun* (Milkweed Editions) and *Tiger Fur* (White Pine Press). Recent books include, from Ecuador, Ana Minga's *Tobacco Dogs* (Bitter Oleander Press, 2013) and Santiago Vizcaino's *Destruction in the Afternoon* (Dialogos Books, 2015) and from Portugal Eugénio de Andrade's *The Art of Patience* (Red Dragonfly Press, 2013) and Sophia de Melo Brynner Andresen's *Exemplary Tales* (Tagus Press, 2015).

Carol Lipszyc's book of poetry, *Singing Me Home,* (2010) and book of short stories on children and adolescents in the Holocaust, *The Saviour Shoes and Other Stories,* (2014) were published by Inanna Publications. Earning her Doctorate in Education at OISE, Carol has published scholarship in arts-based education journals in Australia, New Zealand, England, and Canada. Her Literacy/ESL Reader with chants, *People Express,* was published by Oxford University Press. Carol is currently an Associate Professor in the English Department at SUNY, Plattsburgh where she has contributed as a Poetry Editor to *Saranac Review.*

Malca Litovitz (1952-2005) was the author of three books of poetry: *To Light, To Water* (Lugus Publications, 1998)*; At the Moonbean Café* (Guernica Editions, 2003*);* and *First Day* (Guernica Editions, 2008). With Elana Wolff, she co-authored *Slow Dancing: Creativity and Illness: Duologue and Rengas.* (Guernica Editions, 2008). An endowment for the Malca Litovitz Prize in creative writing was established at Seneca College, Toronto.

Kim Maltman is a poet and theoretical particle physicist who teaches mathematics at York University in Toronto. He is a past winner of the CBC Prize for Poetry. He has published five solo collections of poetry and three collaborative books, including *Introduction to the Introduction to Wang Wei*, written under the pen name Pain Not Bread and published by Brick Books (2000). With Roo Borson, he also writes under the pen name Baziju, whose first book, Box Kite, was published in 2016 by House of Anansi Press.

Mary di Michele is a poet, novelist, and member of the collaborative writing group, Yoko's Dogs. Her books include selected poems, *Stranger in You,* Oxford University Press 1995, and the novel, *Tenor of Love,* Viking Canada, Simon & Schuster USA, 2005. A tenth collection of poetry, *Bicycle Thieves* was published by ECW Press in April 2017. Her awards include first prize for poetry in the CBC literary competition, the Air Canada Writing Award, and the Malahat Review long poem. She lives in Montreal where she teaches at Concordia University.

Campbell McGrath's previous full-length poetry collections are: *In the Kingdom of the Sea Monkeys, Shannon: A Poem of the Lewis and Clark Expedition, Seven Notebooks, Pax Atomica, Florida Poems, Road Atlas: Prose and Other Poems, Spring Comes to Chicago, American Noise,* and *Capitalism.* His awards include the Kingsley Tufts Poetry Award and fellowships from the Guggenheim and MacArthur Foundations. He teaches in the creative writing program at Florida International University in Miami.

Michael Mirolla is the author of four novels, a novella, three short story collections, and three poetry collections. Publications include the novel *Berlin* (a 2010 Bressani Prize winner); and the poetry collection *The House on 14th Avenue* (2014 Bressani Prize). His latest novel *Torp: The Landlord, The Husband, The Wife and The Lover* (Linda Leith Publishing) appeared in 2016. His short story collection *Lessons in Relationship Dyads* (Red Hen Press, 2015) won the 2016 Bressani Prize. Born in Italy and raised in Montreal, Michael now makes his home in the Greater Toronto Area.

Jerry Mirskin has worked as a herdsman on a dairy farm, as a carpenter, and as a New York State Poet-in-the-Schools. He is currently a Professor at Ithaca College and teaches select courses at Cornell University. His first collection, *Picture a Gate Hanging Open and Let that Gate be the Sun*, was published in 2002 after being chosen for first prize in the Mammoth Books Prize for Poetry. His second collection, *In Flagrante Delicto*, was released in November 2008. A collaboration with the photographer, Susan Verberg, entitled *Reflections* was published in 2012. Jerry Mirskin is the winner of the 2013 *Arts & Letters* Prime Poetry Prize. His new collection, *Crepuscular Non Driveway,* was recently published by Mammoth Books.

Jane Munro's sixth poetry collection, *Blue Sonoma* (Brick Books, 2014) won the 2015 Griffin Poetry Prize. Her previous books include *Active Pass* (Pedlar Press, 2010) and *Point No Point* (McClelland & Stewart, 2006). Her work has received the Bliss Carman Poetry Award, the Macmillan Prize for Poetry, was nominated for the Pat Lowther Award and is included in *The Best Canadian Poetry 2013*. She is a member of the collaborative poetry group Yoko's Dogs who have published two collections, *Whisk* (Pedlar Press, 2013) and *Rhinoceros* (Gaspereau, 2016). She lives in Vancouver.

Doug Ramspeck is the author of five poetry collections. His most recent book, *Original Bodies*, was selected for the Michael Waters Poetry Prize and is published by Southern Indiana Review Press. Two earlier books also received awards: *Mechanical Fireflies* (Barrow Street Press Poetry Prize), and *Black Tupelo Country* (John Ciardi Prize, University of Missouri-Kansas City). Individual poems have appeared in journals that include *Kenyon Review, Slate, Southern Review, Georgia Review, AGNI, and Alaska Quarterly Review.* Doug is a two-time recipient of an Ohio Arts Council Individual Excellence Award. He teaches creative writing at The Ohio State University at Lima.

The poetry of **David Reibetanz** has appeared in such periodicals as *The Fiddlehead, The Malahat Review,* and *Descant,* and in the anthologies *In Fine Form* and *Poetry as Liturgy*. His first full book, *Black Suede Cave*, was published in the Fall of 2013 by Guernica Editions. He lives in Toronto, where he teaches English, French, and Yoga.

Matt Robinson's most recent collection is *Some Nights It's Entertainment; Some Other Nights Just Work* (Gaspereau Press, 2016). Previous publications include the chapbook, *a fist made and then un-made* (Gaspereau Press, 2013), which was short-listed for the bpNichol Award, *Against the Hard Angle* (ECW Press, 2010), *no cage contains a stare that well* (ECW Press, 2005), and *A Ruckus of Awkward Stacking* (Insomniac Press, 2000). His poems have won the Petra Kenney Prize, *Grain Magazine's* Prose Poem Award, and *The Malahat Review*'s Long Poem Prize and appeared in anthologies such as *The New Canon, Breathing Fire 2, Coastlines: The Poetry of Atlantic Canada, Exact Fare Only 2,* and *Landmarks: An Anthology of New Atlantic Canadian Poetry of the Land.* He lives in Halifax, NS, with his family and works as the Director of Housing & Conference Services at Saint Mary's University.

Sue Rose works as a literary translator in the UK and has published novels, libretti, plays and poetry in translation. Her debut poetry collection, *From the Dark Room*, was published by Cinnamon Press in 2011. A chapbook, *Heart Archives*, was published by Hercules Editions in February 2014 and a second collection, *The Cost of Keys*, was published by Cinnamon in November 2014. She is currently working on her third collection.

Brynn Saito is the author of two books of poetry, *Power Made Us Swoon* (2016) and *The Palace of Contemplating Departure* (2013), winner of the Benjamin Saltman Poetry Award from Red Hen Press and a finalist for the Northern California Book Award. She also co-authored, with Traci Brimhall, *Bright Power, Dark Peace* (chapbook, Diode Editions). Brynn is a recipient of the Kundiman Asian American Poetry Fellowship and winner of the Key West Literary Seminar's Scotti Merrill Memorial Award. Originally from Fresno, CA, Brynn lives in Los Altos and teaches and works in San Francisco.

Robyn Sarah was born in New York City to Canadian parents and grew up in Montreal, where she still lives. A poet, writer, literary editor, and musician, she is the author of ten poetry collections, most recently *My Shoes Are Killing Me* (Biblioasis, 2015) which won the Governor General's Award for poetry. She has also published two collections of short stories and a book of essays on poetry. Her poems have been broadcast by Garrison Keillor on The Writer's Almanac and anthologized in *The Best Canadian Poetry in English* (2009 and 2010), *The Bedford Introduction to Literature,* and *The Norton Anthology of Poetry.* Since 2011 she has served as poetry editor for Cormorant Books.

Sheryl St. Germain's poetry books include *Making Bread at Midnight, How Heavy the Breath of God, The Journals of Scheherazade,* and *Let it Be a Dark Roux: New and Selected Poems.* She has written two memoirs, *Swamp Songs: the Making of an Unruly Woman,* and *Navigating Disaster: Sixteen Essays of Love and a Poem of Despair.* She co-edited, with Margaret Whitford, *Between Song and Story: Essays for the Twenty-First Century,* and with Sarah Shotland, *Words Without Walls: Writers on Violence, Addiction and Incarceration.* She directs the MFA program in Creative Writing at Chatham University.

Faith Shearin is the author of three books of poetry: *The Owl Question* (May Swenson Award), *The Empty House* (Word Press), and *Moving the*

Piano (SFA University Press). Recent work has appeared in *Alaska Quarterly Review* and *The Southern Review* and has been read aloud by Garrison Keillor on *The Writer's Almanac*. She is the recipient of awards from The Fine Arts Work Center in Provincetown, The Barbara Deming Memorial Fund, and the National Endowment for the Arts. Her work also appears in *The Autumn House Anthology of Contemporary Poets* and in *Good Poems, American Places*. She lives with her husband, her daughter, and a small, opinionated dachshund, in a cabin on top of a mountain in West Virginia.

Kenneth Sherman is a Toronto poet and essayist. His most recent books are *Wait Time: A Memoir of Cancer*, published by Wilfred Laurier University, 2015, the long poem, *Black River*, and, *What the Furies Bring*, a collection of essays, which won the Canadian Jewish Book Award.

David R. Slavitt is a poet, novelist, critic and translator who has published more than 100 works of literature across genres. Recipient of national awards for translation and literature, his collections of poetry include *The Odes of Horace* (University of Wisconsin Press 2014), *Civil Wars* (Louisiana State University Press 2013), and *PS 3569. L3*(1998), and *Dozens* (1981).

Carolyn Smart's sixth collection of poems, *Careen,* was published in 2015 from Brick Books. An excerpt from her memoir *At the End of the Day* (Penumbra Press, 2001) won first prize in the 1993 CBC Literary Contest, and her narrative poetry collection *Hooked* has been performed at the Edinburgh and Seattle Fringe Festivals. She is the founder of the RBC Bronwen Wallace Award for Emerging Writers, and since 1989 has been Director of Creative Writing at Queen's University.

Gillian Sze is the author of eight poetry collections, including *Fish Bones* (DC Books, 2009), which was shortlisted for the QWF McAuslan First Book Prize, and *Peeling Rambutan* (Gaspereau Press, 2014), which was shortlisted for the QWF A.M. Klein Prize for Poetry. Her work has received awards such as the University of Winnipeg Writers' Circle Prize and the 2011 3Macs carte blanche Prize. She studied Creative Writing and English Literature and received a Ph.D. in Études anglaises from Université de Montréal. Her latest works include the chapbook, *Fricatives* (Gaspereau Press, 2015), and *Redrafting Winter* (BuschekBooks, 2015), a collaborative book of poems and letters.

Ernő Szép (1884-1953) was a prolific Hungarian lyric poet, journalist, dramatist and novelist of great popularity and renown. Born in Huszt, a town now in the Ukraine, his verse has been characterized as representing the "Impressionist" style. In addition to his poetry, Szép's works include the plays *Patika* (Pharmacy, 1918) and *A vőlegény* (The Bridegroom, 1922), as well as the novel *Lila akác* (Wisteria, 1921) which served as the basis of films in 1934 and 1972. Szép is perhaps best known for his last published work, *Emberszag* (The Smell of Humans: A Memoir of the Holocaust in Hungary). The annual Szép Ernő Prize was inaugurated in 1984 to recognize singular achievements by Hungarian dramatists.

Eva M. Thury is currently completing a translation of *Egy Lépés Jeruzsálem Felé*, by Sándor Bacskai, a work based on ethnographies of Orthodox Jewish life in Hungary after the second World War. She is co-author of *Introduction to Mythology Contemporary Approaches to Classical and World Myths*, 4th ed. (Oxford 2016) with Margaret K. Devinney. Thury is an Associate Professor of English at Drexel University and was a Senior Editor of the *Drexel Online Journal*, writing "with a small 'c,'" a column on contemporary culture. She is an Associate Contributor to *When Falls the Coliseum*, with "Stone Age Memes," on the foibles of the digital age.

Eva Tihanyi was born in Budapest, Hungary, in 1956 and came to Canada when she was six. She has taught at Niagara College since 1989 and divides her time between Toronto and Port Dalhousie (St. Catharines, Ontario). She has published eight books of poetry and one collection of short stories (*Truth and Other Fictions*, Inanna, 2009). Her most recent books are *The Largeness of Rescue* (Inanna, 2016) and *Flying Underwater: Poems New and Selected* (Inanna, 2012).

Lewis Turco is the author of *The Book of Forms: A Handbook of Poetics*, originally published in 1968 and currently in its fourth edition, plus many other books in various genres. His most recent is an epic, *The Hero Enkidu*, published by Bordighera Press (2015).

Tamar Yoseloff's fifth collection, *The Formula for Night: New and Selected Poems* was published by Seren in 2015. She is also the author of *Formerly*, a chapbook incorporating photographs by Vici MacDonald (Hercules Editions, 2012), which was shortlisted for the Ted Hughes Award for New Work in Poetry; three collaborative editions with artists (*Marks* and *Desire Paths*, with Linda Karshan; and *Nowheres* with David Harker). She lives in London where she is a freelance tutor of creative writing, often combining poetry and the visual arts in courses for galleries such as the Royal Academy and the Hayward.

Patricia Young has published thirteen collections of poetry, two of which have been shortlisted for the Governor General's Award. She has also received the Pat Lowther Award, the Dorothy Livesay Award, several National Magazine Awards and the CBC Literary Award. *Airstream*, her collection of short fiction won the Rooke-Metcalf Award and was named one of the *Globe and Mail*'s Best Books of the Year.

Printed in August 2017
by Gauvin Press,
Gatineau, Québec